CREDIT SECRETS

2 BOOKS IN 1

Learn How to Repair Your Profile
and Fix your Debt.
Boost Your Score Rapidly,
In A Simple, Legal and Effective Way.
609 Letter Templates Included.

By: Dave Rich

BUNDLE CONTENT

CREDIT REPAIR SECRETS

A Simple and Detailed Guide to Learn Strategies to Repair Your Negative Profile. Discover the Best Tricks of Credit Lawyers to Fix Your Bad Debt.

CREDIT SCORE SECRETS

Improve Your Business or Personal Finance with This Ultimate Guide to Boost Your Credit Score.
Learn How to Manage Your Money and Change Your Mindset in Few Easy Steps.

BONUS CHAPTER

609 Templates

professional before attempting any techniques outlined in this book.

By reading this document, the reader agrees that under no circumstances is the author responsible for any losses, direct or indirect, which are incurred as a result of the use of information contained within this document, including, but not limited to, — errors, omissions, or inaccuracies.

CREDIT REPAIR SECRETS

A Simple and Detailed Guide
to Learn Strategies to
Repair Your Negative Profile.
Discover the Best Tricks of
Credit Lawyers to Fix Your
Bad Debt.

By: Dave Rich

TABLE OF CONTENTS

INTRODUCTION

Most of us know that a poor credit score can prevent us from getting a loan or a credit card, but many of us don't know that it can also affect other areas of our lives such as: A poor credit score can prevent you from getting a job or a promotion. Employers are permitted by federal and many state laws to use your credit history in hiring decisions, believing that how someone handles their financial responsibilities is an indication of how well they might handle their work responsibilities as well.

Many people become enthusiastic about credit repairing and when they see the effort involved and the time required on the journey to good credit, they get discouraged and give up. Others give up after the first negative response from a creditor or credit report agency and some even go through with it but stop doing things to improve their credit when they've finished the process and still haven't managed to fix all the negative items. The important thing about the whole process is to stay motivated and continue improving. It is going to be extremely important throughout your life so that you can have fun and do the things you enjoy.

How much your credit status affects insurance is somewhat dependent on state laws. Your credit status may affect your rates or types of homeowner, rental, or car insurance. Some auto insurance companies believe that poor credit correlates to a higher accident risk and require higher premiums.

Buying a home is a big step and unless you can pay for it in cash, you will need a loan. This means everything involved comes down to your credit score and credit report. They will determine if you can even get a loan. If you can get a loan, they will determine the amount, type, and interest rate of the loan. It may also affect purchases you never thought about such as your homeowner's insurance, and necessities for the home such buying a refrigerator or a bed on credit.

The better your personal credit status is, the better chance you have of getting a start-up loan or a loan to expand your business. Most investors and lenders want to be confident in the financial status of the principals in the company, in particular their credit status. The theory being that if you cannot manage your own finances, how can you handle those of a business? Also, if you are selling a product and your credit status is good, the manufacturer of the product may be more likely to front you the product and allow you to pay for it after.

In fact, poor credit can easily cost you thousands of dollars a year in higher interest, larger fees, bigger premiums, extra loan points, and other hidden costs. Not only will that, but a single negative item on your credit report haunt you for years. On the other hand, having a high score will get you credit when and where you need it. It increases your chances for landing better jobs, getting lower interest rates and fees. This is not only convenient but can save you thousands of dollars over a period of time.

More reasons, a poor credit score can keep you from renewing a professional license or prevent you from getting utilities or cable connections in your new apartment/home. It can also prevent you from posting bail for yourself or someone else. There are literally hundreds of ways a poor credit score can negatively impact your life, and what is more, it can do so for years to come, if you do not act on it.

Now, let us understand the basics of credit repair.

CREDIT REPAIR SECRET

Basic of Credit Repair

Credit repair is the process in which credit standing is fixed, which might have declined due to various reasons. Credit standing might be as straightforward as disputing the information.

Another kind of credit fix is to take care of financial problems such as budgeting and start to deal with concerns.

Credit repair is the action of repairing or restoring a bad credit rating, Credit repair may also entail paying a company to get in touch with the credit agency and point out anything in your report that is untrue or incorrect, then requesting this to be eliminated.

It is hard to navigate today's society using credit. A variety of companies use your credit to choose also to place the pricing for services and goods that you use and also whether to do business. Consumers using a credit history seek out credit repair to increase their credit to have a simpler time.

By making your financial goals, setting your budget, finding ways to save money, and requesting a copy of your credit report, you have done your preliminary legwork in trying to get your finances back in order.

What is Bad Credit?

Bad credit is when you have missed one or more payments throughout your life, be it your fault or not. The most common mistake people make is not defaulting on a payment, it is actually delaying payments. It is usually when you forget about a deadline or can't find a certain bill and you end up not paying, or being late, which in the eyes of the people borrowing money makes you look a bit financially unstable. Sometimes, even if you have had impeccable behavior, you are unfortunately affected by the loss of a job. Becoming unemployed has such grave consequences and lead to your assets being repossessed or even bankruptcy. Even if you went through a similar phase and you have bounced back, having this kind of history will impact your credit report in a negative way for a very long period of time.

It can also happen to you to be the victim of an error, even if you have not missed a single payment on your credit card until now. An error in the bank's system or an error from the parties responsible for building your credit report will affect you nonetheless, and so will fraud and abuse. Fraud cases are rare, but their consequences are costly. Fraud happens when someone uses your identity to submit a credit application, they get it and then they do not repay it anymore. You will be contacted by the bank and until you can prove you have been the target of a scam; you can have a tough time. Abuse generally refers to when you are oblivious with your expenses and spend over your credit card limit. You can wake up one day to a huge amount of debt and cases of abuse most often end in you being forced to declare bankruptcy. In order to avoid these cases, you need to be very careful with your finances, but regardless of what your situation is, usually there is a solution or a set of measures you can enforce to prevent it.

REPAIR CREDIT SOLUTION

B y making your financial goals, setting your budget, finding ways to save money, and requesting a copy of your credit report, you've done your preliminary legwork in trying to get your finances back in order.

Now that all three credit reporting agencies have a copy of your credit report, it's time to roll up your sleeves and tackle the inaccurate information reported on your credit report.

Reviewing Your Credit Report

When you check each of your credit reports, whether it is on the website of the credit reporting agency where you can download it, or a hard copy of your report which you received in the mail, it is vital that each entry is accurately reported.

When you consider misleading or incorrect information on the credit report, the Equal Credit Reporting Act notes you have the right to dispute the submission with the credit reporting agency. The credit reporting agency has to re-examine the creditor's admission. The enquiry must be concluded within 30 days of receiving the lawsuit message.

If the borrower fails to respond within that time period, the credit reporting agency must delete from the credit report the entry you are contesting. If the creditor replies and the inaccurate entry are corrected, the credit reporting agency will update your credit report. There is also the risk that the borrower can respond to the credit report and not make any changes in it. If you're not happy with your revised credit report, you should write a 100-word paragraph to clarify your side of the story on any of the remaining items on the credit report. This customer statement will then surface any time it appears on your credit report. If you don't want to write a 100-word paragraph on your credit report, you will be able to write another 120-day appeal letter from your most recent credit report.

When you access your credit report on the Website of the credit reporting agency, you will be able to dispute the incorrect entries online. The site will have boxes to check for inaccuracy alongside an appropriate reason. If you choose to write a personalized message, you can also use the same answers as appropriate. Sample answers would be:

- This is not my account.
- This was not late as indicated.
- This was not charged off.
- This was paid off in full as agreed.
- This was not a collection account.
- This is not my bankruptcy as indicated.
- This is not my tax lien as indicated.
- This is not my judgment as indicated.

What you shouldn't do:

- Alter your identity, or try to change it.
- The story is fictional.
- Check any information which is 100% correct.

What you should do:

- Read your emails, should you decide to send them to us. If a letter looks legitimate, credit reporting agencies will believe it has been written by a credit repair service, and they will not investigate the dispute.
- Use your original letterhead (if you do have one).

- Use the appeal form included with the credit report by the credit reporting agency, if you want.
- Provide some evidence suggesting the wrong entry is erroneous.
- Include the identification number for all communications listed on the credit report.

Common Credit Report Errors

Note, there could be various mistakes in each of the three credit reports. It is not uncommon to have positive coverage of an account on one article, but poor reports on another.

Here are some of the most common credit report errors.

- Listed wrong names, emails, or phone numbers.
- Data that refers to another of the same name.
- Duplicate details, whether positive or negative, about the same account.
- Records have negative, apparently positive information.
- Balances on accounts payable are still on view.
- Delinquent payment reports that were never billed in due time.
- This indicates wrong credit limits.
- Claims included in the insolvency which are still due.
- Incorrect activity dates;

- Past-due payments not payable.
- Court records which are falsely connected with you, such as convictions and bankruptcy.
- Tax liens not yours.
- Unprecedented foreclosures.

Spotting Possible Identity Theft

Checking your credit report could also spot potential identity theft. That's why you should inquire at least once a year or every six months for a copy of your credit report.

Things to look for would be:

- Names of accounts and figures that you do not know.
- You don't remember filling out loan applications.
- Addresses you didn't live in.
- Poor bosses or tenants' enquiries you don't know.

Creditors Can Help

Many times, if you have had a long-term account with a creditor, you can contact them directly and explain the error being reported on your credit report.

Ask them to write you a letter with the email and correction. Also ask them to contact every credit reporting agency that reports this incorrect entry in order to make the correction.

Once the creditor receives a copy of the letter, make a copy of it and attach the letter to the letter of dispute you send. Mail it to the agency for credit reporting, and ask them to update their files. Once that is completed, you will be sent back a new credit report by the credit reporting agency.

Credit Rescoring

Rapid rescoring is an expedited way of fixing anomalies in the credit file of a customer. The bad news is, you can't do it yourself. A fast rescore dispute process works through borrowers and mortgage brokers, a number of approved registry credit reporting companies, and credit reporting agencies.

If you are a creditor applying for a rescore on your credit report, you would need to provide detailed documents that would be sent to the collateral agencies that are working on your case. Cash registry is the system used by cash grantors. The data archive gathers the records from the three main credit reporting agencies, and has to check the consumer's initial information for a rescore. Once the verification is entered into the program of the repository a new score will be produced.

The key thing to keep in mind is that a simple rescore can only be temporary. You may be able to close a loan with it, but you must follow through on your credit report with the three main credit reporting firms to ensure it has been removed or corrected. If it reappears, forward the reports immediately to credit reporting agencies.

The downside of a fast rescore is that you save money without having to contend individually with a credit reporting agency that may take longer than 30 days to complete an audit. If the sale of a house or lease depends on your credit score, and you're in a time crunch, the best solution is to easily rescore.

Should You Use a Credit Repair Company?

Using a credit repair company's services is basically hiring a firm to do what you can do for yourself. The process is really without secrets. All the credit repair company does is dispute information on negative entries on your credit report with credit reporting agencies. Most companies may report having agreements with credit reporting agencies or have a secret way to get borrowers to delete unfavorable entries. This is more than likely not true because both state and federal laws under the Fair Credit Reporting Act regulate the credit reporting agencies.

You will be charged a fee for working with a credit repair company. Many systems will call up your credit records or allow you to access your own reports. The letter-writing campaign starts after you have entered into a contract with the firm.

The reason some people hire an outsourced credit repair company is because they feel intimidated or have no time to do the work themselves. Until signing up with a credit repair company there are many steps you need to take. Many businesses operate illegally and you don't want to get caught in that trap.

Beware of Credit Repair Scams

Sadly, it is easy for people to fall prey to credit repair fraud when they are vulnerable and are going through financial challenges. If you're looking for a repair company for cash, here's how to say if it's a genuine or scam business. Many scam firms may only sign up to take the money and run for their services. This is a list of stuff that should raise a red flag.

The company wants you to pay for credit repair services before it provides any services.

- The company doesn't tell you your rights, and you can do it for free. This should appear in any document it presents you with.
- The firm advises that you do not explicitly approach any of the three major national credit reporting agencies. It knows that if you do, you may learn that it took your money, and that it does nothing.
- The company tells you that even if that information is accurate, it can get rid of all the negative credit reports

in your credit report. No one can promise just one thing on your credit report for change.

- The company assumes you're trying to create a "different" credit identifier. This is known as file segregation. It is accomplished by filing for the use of an Employer Identification Number to create a new credit report instead of the Social Security number. That is utterly unconstitutional.

- The firm encourages you to challenge any information contained in your credit report regardless of accuracy or timeliness of the material. If the evidence is 100% right, then you have no basis for a disagreement.

Remember, if you are given unlawful advice and follow it knowing it is illegal, you may be committing fraud, and you will find yourself in lawful hot water.

If you use the postal, mobile, or Internet to apply for credit and provide false information, you could be charged and prosecuted with mail or wire fraud. Most of the programs you sign on have a promise that the details you receive are valid when signing the contract.

The Credit Service Organizations Act

Credit repair facilities are governed under State and Federal law by the Credit Service Organizations Act. Under this act, most states require that credit repair companies in each state where they do business be registered and bonded. There are different requirements for each Country. When signing up for this program you will check a copy of your state's Credit Service Organizations Act. The Federal Trade Commission and the offices of the State Attorney General are going after credit repair companies that do not comply with the regulations and are soliciting customers with misleading information. Through visiting: www.ftc.gov, you can also get a copy of the state edition of the Credit Service Organizations Act.

Some of this law's key provisions are for consumer protection by signing up with a credit repair service. A credit repair company must give you a written contract that outlines your rights and obligations that its state has approved. Make sure to read the paperwork before signing something. So know that a credit repair company can't:

- Make false claims about its facilities, before signing.
- Charge yourself until the promised services are complete.
- Provide certain activities until a formal contract has been signed and a three-day waiting period has been fulfilled. You will cancel the contract during this period, without paying any fees.

STEPS TO REPAIR BAD CREDIT

Step 1- Get Your Credit Report

This step is crucial; banks and similar credit bureaus, which in turn hold the key to repairing the credit, report all credit information. Most people never consider getting their credit reports until they are trying to repair the credit, but it's always a good idea.

In most cases, there should be no charge for receiving a copy of your credit report; you simply have to request it (usually in writing, in person and accompanied by a copy of your identification). When you are considered a bad creditor for a credit card or loan, the company must indicate which credit bureau reported you as having bad credit, and then you can request a report from that bureau. Credit repair begins with a detailed look at your credit report. Look for any inaccuracies: in some cases, they may be errors in your file, or your credit information may be mistaken for someone else with the same name. If you find any inaccuracies, you can repair your credit by applying in writing to the credit bureau. If you have any supporting documentation, include it, otherwise simply indicate where the confusion is and request that it be analyzed. This benefits you in two ways: first, if the credit bureau cannot verify the information you are disputing, by default it must be deleted from your file; second, if the bureau does not respond to your request for investigation within 30 days, the disputed information must be deleted.

If it turns out that your bad credit is the result of an error, you should usually go to the credit bureau, that's all you need to do to repair the credit. When you order your credit report, keep in mind that your processors will make the process seem more difficult than it is, since in terms of hours they are not interested in responding to many requests for credit reports.

Step 2- Contact your Bank Agency

Once you went over your credit report and determined that everything is correct, the next step in repairing your credit history is to contact creditors with whom you have delinquent accounts. You should repair these accounts as soon as possible to successfully repair your credit.

In many cases, the creditor's priority is to recover as much of the account receivable as possible. Many people are surprised at how accommodating they can be in terms of organizing a payment process: in many cases, the creditor will eliminate interest or even reduce the bill and return it for immediate payment. If you can't pay immediately, propose a payment plan for the creditor that you can stick to: Creditors will accommodate most payment proposals because, again, your primary interest will be to recover the debt.

Remember that the reason you're doing this is to repair your credit history, so under no circumstances should you commit to a payment plan with your creditors that you won't be able to meet would only end up making problems worse in the future. If a creditor has repeated problems with a client, it is unlikely that there is much trust in the relationship, so they probably won't want to help you. Instead, choose something you can meet and explain your current financial situation to the creditor. By doing this, you can often achieve credit repair quickly.

Step 3- Try and Avoid the Collection Agency

The worst and last step a creditor will take is to sell your outstanding debt to a collection agency. In terms of credit repair, this is the worst thing that can happen because it means that whomever you owed money to consider your chances of recovering it so low that you are willing to lose some of the debt. In most cases, the creditor sells the debt to the collection agency at a large discount, often half the amount owed.

When a debtor sold his loan to a collection agency, he just "canceled" it and created the lowest possible mark on his credit history. If this happens, try and act as soon as possible after being contacted by the collection agent. Before you negotiate with the collection company, talk to your creditor. See if the creditor will remove the "canceled" mark from your credit history. This is something they will do sometimes, in exchange for an immediate payment.

If your creditor is not interested in negotiating payment, you would be in trouble with the collection agent. It can and will happen that the debt collector stays in a very intimidating and threatening position, usually implying that they are willing to take you to trial. The two points to keep in mind is that the collection company bought your debt for less than the amount owed, and you are unlikely to be sued. Your best solution is to offer to make an immediate payment for less than the actual balance of your debt. Most companies will accept this, usually because making a profit on any payment that exceeds 50% of their debt and offering to pay immediately allows them to close their file and work on other issues. When dealing with a collection agent, only offer full payment as a last resort.

Step 4- Apply for a Secured Credit Card

Credit repair can be a slow process, and you may find yourself building a bit of credit backing slowly over a long period of time. A good place to start is with a "secured" credit card. These credit cards are issued by banking agencies that generally target people who have bad credit. Unlike a regular credit card, for which you will no doubt be rejected if you have a bad credit, it is a secured credit; the card usually requires you to give an initial deposit equivalent to the credit limit of the card. That is, you give the company $500 for a card with a credit limit of $500, and they reserve the right to use that deposit against any outstanding balance that remains for too long.

From the issuer's point of view, their bad credit won't matter because they don't take any risk: you'll never owe them more money than you've already given them to start with. From your point of view, secured cards are far from ideal, but if you have bad credit and need to participate in credit repair, you have no choice.

Once you have a secured credit card, use it sparingly but regularly, and are sure to make all your payments on time. By doing this over a long period of time, you will slowly repair your credit history and regain the confidence of creditors who rejected you in the past.

Step 5- Consider a Company that Specializes in Credit Repair

If you find that none of the above works for you in terms of credit repair, consider going to a company that specializes in this type of process. Many of these companies will offer to "clean up your credit record" for a fee. While the services of a credit repair company can be much more helpful, depending on your situation, you must be very careful to avoid scams and read all the fine print that is in most cases.

The basic strategy of most credit repair companies will be to encourage you to claim absolutely everything on your credit report with your credit bureau. The idea is to flood the office with more requests than they can respond to within 30 days, because remember that if the office can't provide documentation for something in your file within 30 days, it must be remote.

However, it is questionable how effective this really is, although the office, if it does not document them, must remove items within 30 days, in most cases companies will continue to investigate the claims, and when they finally find the proper documentation, the items will be added again.

Whatever you decide regarding a credit repair company, always remember to go over the documents carefully. Also, note that credit repair companies cannot legally accept payments until services are completed. They are also required to clearly describe all payments and terms.

THE BASIC OF CREDIT CARD DEBT AND BANKRUPTCY

People know the basics about credit cards. Once you are approved, you then receive your card and activate it. You can use it for pretty much anything, such as for purchasing groceries, clothing, or for paying bills. The nice part is that you only have to make the minimum payment every month to keep yourself out of credit card debt. Unfortunately, it is this kind of thinking that often leads people into credit card debt.

Below are some basic points that most people don't realize about credit card debt.

1. Know when short-term loans make more sense

Sometimes we need to get some cash or find a way to pay a few bills quickly. Many people turn to credit cards for these reasons. They receive their answer within minutes and their card will arrive in the mail in about five to seven business days. However, sometimes it is better to go to your bank and talk to a loan advisor instead. If you need a couple thousand dollars in order to pay off your medical bills so they aren't sent to a collection agency, it might be best to take out a short-term loan from your local bank or credit union.

2. Credit card debt can result in bad credit

Paying off your credit cards in a less than timely manner or missing the minimum payment aren't the only things that are going to result in your having bad credit; having credit cards that hold high balances can also increase your chances of bad credit. In fact, you should make sure you always have at least 30 percent of your credit limit available.

While it is almost impossible in today's world, your best chance of keeping yourself from having bad credit is by remaining as free of debt as you possibly can.

3. Owing is the easy part, and the hard part is paying credit cards back

The reality of life is that you never really know what is going to happen. You could have a job for a couple of decades and then find out that you are randomly laid off due to cutbacks. You could have an illness spike that causes surgery. There are a lot of situations that can cause you to think you can start paying your credit cards every other month so you can make other bills. You could also find yourself struggling to pay the full minimum balance, so you may decide to pay about half of it every month.

Another reason your debt will climb is due to your credit limit increasing. This makes you feel mentally secure about being able to purchase your new couch on your credit card because your limit just increased $500. However, what you are really doing is creating more credit card debt and causing your minimum monthly payment to increase. On top of this, your interest is going to compound, which makes it increase.

4. You will find yourself spending more than you make

It doesn't matter how responsible you are with credit cards; one of the biggest reasons people find themselves in credit card debt is because they spend more than they make every month. Credit cards are very tempting because they provide you with the thought that you can just pay it back later or make smaller payments on the purchase every month. Although, in reality, you should never spend more than what your monthly income is.

5. Most people use credit cards to handle emergencies

It is common for people to tell others that a credit card is only used for emergencies, but do you really keep in mind what a true emergency is? Most people live paycheck to paycheck. Therefore, when they see their checking account balance drop low and there are several days before their next payday, they will start to think about each purchase they make and wonder if they should use their credit card as it is considered an emergency or a need

6. People think as long as they make the minimum payment they will be fine

In reality, you always want to make sure you pay more than the minimum payment. Think of it this way: if you have a $75 minimum payment, at least 25 percent of what you pay is going to go toward interest and fees. This means that you are really only putting 75 percent of your payment toward paying off your debt. Depending on how you much you owe, this could be a low amount. If you aren't careful, you could find yourself going over your credit limit, which means your credit card company will charge you their over-the-limit fee.

Furthermore, only paying the minimum payment is going to take you years to pay off. It really doesn't matter how low you feel your credit limit is versus how high you believe your minimum monthly payment is. It can still take at least a couple of years to pay off your debt, providing you stop using your credit card.

Bankruptcy

Only an organization or individual that is unable to completely honor its financial obligation or make payment to its creditor files for bankruptcy. This goes to say that a bankruptcy filing is a legal course of action taken by a company or person to relieve themselves from debt obligations where all outstanding debt of the company is evaluated and paid from the company's assets. As legal proceeding goes, bankruptcy is carried out to give individuals and businesses freedom from debt they have already incurred and at the same time provide creditors with the opportunity to get their debts paid. It can be said to allow for a fresh start by forgiving debts that cannot be paid and at the same time offering creditors a substantive opportunity to get methods of repayment based on the available assets of a person or business that can be liquidated.

Theoretically, this can mean that the ability to file for bankruptcy can benefit a whole economy by giving businesses and individuals a second chance to have the utmost access to consumer credit and by providing creditors with a reliable measure of debt repayment. Once there is the successful completion of a bankruptcy proceeding, the debtor is to be relieved of their obligation from the debt that has been incurred before filing for bankruptcy. However, it will be on their credit record that such a person has acquired debts before and filed for bankruptcy. This information is going to remain on the record for about seven to ten years depending on the type of bankruptcy filed.

Types of Bankruptcy

There are two types of bankruptcy.

1. Debt Discharge: This is simply the cancellation of debt, thanks to bankruptcy. Based on the Internal Revenue Code, a debtor must add into their gross income, the discharge of indebtedness after which a court must have discharged his/her debt upon meeting all conditions. However, if a debtor should refuse financial counseling, commits a crime, fail to fully explain the loss of his/her assets, provide false information during court proceedings or basically disobey the orders of the court, a judge can rightfully refuse to discharge the debt of such a person.

2. The Payment Plan: This is a kind of bankruptcy filed, where a debtor and his/her lawyer submit to the court, a kind of repayment plan of how the debtor plans to pay off his/her debts in three to five years. This plan is dependent on the debtor's income, food, and utilities, tax, and healthcare expenses. Should the court approve the plan, the debtor proceeds to make the payments required as stipulated in the

plan. If such a debtor is consistent with the payments, the remaining debts at the end of the three to five-year period will be discharged. The payments are made to a trustee from the bankruptcy court that then proceeds to pay the creditors while getting a commission too.

Concerning business, the two types of bankruptcy are;

- Reorganization Bankruptcy: This is a kind of bankruptcy filed which is meant to help business owners who have serious issues with their business but still have regular income and valuable assets, reorganize the business. The business is allowed to continue its operations with the court's supervision of course. The creditors aren't allowed to interfere with the debtors during the supervision. Business owners will have to share their reorganization plan with the creditors providing them part of the payment. But if the creditors do not agree with the plan, they have the right to file a competing plan.
- Farming Bankruptcy: It is a type of bankruptcy specially designed for farmers of the same family. It is to help the family reorganize their farming business as well as settle all their debts. The unpredictable nature of farming and seasonal moods is factors that are seriously considered.

Implications of Bankruptcy

Before you consider filing for bankruptcy, you need to first understand how it works as well as the pros and cons. It's not a simple issue that can be done quickly but has a complex side only a bankruptcy attorney understands. It would be best if you find out everything you can before filing for bankruptcy. Find below the consequences of filing a bankruptcy.

Pros:

- Discharge: Getting debts discharged is one major reason people file for bankruptcy. And when such debt is discharged, erasing all your debts as well as preventing creditors from collecting further payments from you, the debtor becomes relieved. It's one huge advantage of filing for bankruptcy. Not everyone who filed for debt discharge is granted. If you owe debts on alimony, tax liabilities or child support, filing for bankruptcy would be a waste of time. Such debts are not forgiven nor discharged.

- Automatic Stay: Here is another advantage to be enjoyed when a bankruptcy is filed. It is a situation whereby the person who files for bankruptcy becomes automatically protected from the creditors, as well as the property over the collection of debts. The protection stays until the court finally decrees the debts to be honored and forgiven or discharged. In a situation that involves divorce proceedings, the automatic stay might be lifted.

Cons

- Loss of Property: There's a possibility that a bankruptcy filer might lose his property if the court decides its valuable enough to pay off the debt owed. This would happen if you include your property in

36

your case to the bankruptcy trustee. Your creditor will have higher leverage in trying to get your property especially if you used such property initially as collateral.

- Credit Score: Another downside to filing for bankruptcy is that it decreases your credit score. Loaners will only see you as risky when they check your credit history because filing for bankruptcy won't in any way clean up your debt history even though your debt is canceled. However, it's a better option than acquiring debt. You can always rebuild your credit score later.

- Privacy: If you're sensitive about your privacy, filing for bankruptcy might not be for you, and this explains why you must make your research if you want to file for bankruptcy. You can either prepare yourself against the consequences or look for other options. When you file a bankruptcy case, every detail about your financial statements becomes public. In other words, anyone can access your personal information without your permission. The amount you owed, who your creditors were, and your bankruptcy schedule can be assessed easily by anyone. It can be such a big deal if you cherish your privacy.

HOW TO PAY OFF A DEBT

Remember that you need to focus on paying off all your debts at the earliest. You cannot waste any more time and must try and finish them off to have a good score. Let us now look at the things that you need to do to pay off your debts on time.

You can pay off your debts in one of the two methods that are made available viz. the first one being the avalanche method and the second being the snowball method. Each type has its own advantages and disadvantages. You need to look at whatever fits your budget best and go for it without wasting any more time. If you think you have enough money saved up then choose the avalanche method but if you have very little then chose the snowballing method. Apart from these, if you have enough money to pay everything all together then you can choose that option as well.

Planning

Remember to always work with a plan. When you have everything planned out it will be easy for you to finish your task. Start by preparing a monthly budget by including your incomes and expenses and try and balance it out to remain with as much money at the end as possible. You need to add your debts to the expenses column and this will help you pay them on time. When you are left with a surplus, you can use it to open a separate "debt repayment" account and add in the money there. Once you have a substantial amount, you can use it to pay off all your debts.

Organizing

Mere planning will not suffice and you need to be as organized as possible. You must have everything in place to help you operate smoothly. Try having a different account for each of your debts so that money automatically gets transferred every month. You must also have a set monthly budget for your expenses. You must not use any more money than what you have assigned. When you are organized, you will feel that your life is easy and there are not many obstacles standing in your way.

Contact

The next step is to contact your creditors. This means that you get in touch with them and assure them that you are going to pay your debts on time. Many times, it pays to develop a good rapport with your creditors. But don't push it and remain within your limits. You need to develop a rapport and not a close friendship with them. You need to win over their trust and make them like your determination. Remain in touch with them and update them on your every move to repay their debts on time. After a while, the informality between the two of you will start to reduce.

Negotiate

When you have struck a good rapport, you can decide to ask for a small rebate in your debt or negotiate the rate of interest that you have to pay. This might not be possible with all creditors such as banks but you can try your luck with moneylenders and other non-commercial lenders. Once they are happy with your timely debt repayments, they might decide to reduce the interest rate by a little. But don't expect them to waive off your loan as nobody will be willing to do that. You can ask them if you can pay a little less for the last few installments and count that as your rebate.

Secured credit card

When you are trying to pay off all your debts at the earliest, you must not use your credit card excessively. Your credit score will plummet and so, it is best that you give up on these. There are alternatives to credit cards that you can consider. Debit cards are a great idea as you will only draw money from your own account when you use these. Buy if you want to have the feel of a credit card then you can opt for a secured credit card. These are issued by your bank and they will be linked to your account. You will have to add money to this account and there will be a limit on how much you can draw in a month. There will be no interest levied on the amount and you must add back the money that you withdrew within a specified period of time to help the account remain active.

Family

Sometimes, if there is a lot of debt then you can consider borrowing some money from your relatives. When you do so, you will be able to pay off a debt easily. Your family members might not charge you a high rate of interest and it might be within your budget. You can consider asking your dad or your uncle or anybody who is in a position to pay you the amount at the earliest. You need not stress over paying the sum back to them and can do it leisurely and at your own pace.

Life insurance

It is also possible for you to borrow money from your life insurance policy. You can ask for a certain amount that you promise to pay back within a specified period of time. There is no interest as such that will be levied on this sum and you can repay it after a few years' time. Once you repay your debt and give back to your insurance company then you will truly be free and your credit score will start to rise high.

Bank borrowing

It pays to have everything unified to make for easy payments. This means that you can borrow a certain amount from your bank and pay off all your creditors in bulk. You can then pay only to your bank to settle your debts. This will make it easier for you as you have to pay to only one institution. The rate of interest might also be low and that will help you save on a lot of money. The only disadvantage of this type is that, not many banks entertain this sort of borrowing. However, you can try your luck and approach two or more banks with a proposal.

Money savers

Every month, think of ways in which you can save on money. This can be by way of using coupons while shopping or making use of store credit to help save on the bill etc. You can also sell your old and unused stuff to make some money out of it. It is also a good idea to gift a service instead of a physical gift as this will further help you in saving money. Nevertheless, if you cannot gift a service every time then you can consider buying them in bulk after the holiday is over and store it to be gifted the next year. Cutting down on electricity, water and gas bills will also help you save money. It is also ideal for you to buy second hand goods for the time being and save further.

You can follow these steps to repay all your loans at the earliest and improve your credit score.

CONSEQUENCES OF NOT PAYING OFF YOUR DEBT

What happens when you go into serious delinquency or default on your loans? Well, it depends on the type of loan. With cars and houses, they can be repossessed by the bank. With consumer debt, you are often going to have to declare bankruptcy to wipe out old debts if you are far enough underwater.

Government-backed student loans, however, are a whole different beast. They can NOT be removed via bankruptcy. After 270 days of no payments, they are officially in default and sit there like a bad acne breakout on your credit report, making your score look yucky. Some student loan companies will then turn the loans over to official debt collection companies, which start yammering your phone away about late payments. In addition, you'll be on the hook for their own special fees. Yay.

You might have to try the 'secured credit card' trick to build up your credit again after this kind of financial disaster. Some people want to reach out to a debt settlement company or try to get a payday loan, but please don't! Debt settlement companies have to get paid too, you know, and they'll come after your money one way or another. Most of them are scams. The only honest ones are nonprofits, and even those are doubtful. Payday loans charge sickening interest rates of more than 500% in some cases, so for a $1,000 payday loan, you'll be screwed out of more than $5,000. What kind of sense does that make? Stay far away from them.

If you don't pay your credit cards, they sit untouched with the original creditor for about six months. An original creditor is a bank like Chase, Citi, Capital One, Discover, or American Express. If you keep making payments, even if it's just $10 a month, the account will remain open with the original creditor.

But if you stop making payments for six months, then the original creditor turns the debt along with its collected interest over to a debt collection company. They then attempt to collect the debt for another six months. By now, you've not made a single payment for a year. If no payments are made, then your debt, with any added fees and other expenses from the debt collection company, is then turned over to a law office, where a judgment is brought against you in the form of a lawsuit. The law office represents either the original creditor or the debt buying company. The number of small claims lawsuits based on collecting past debts has increased significantly in the past ten years, and now there are specialty law firms devoted solely to debt collecting from average people. Well, at least we don't have debtors' prisons anymore.

If this happens, the creditor or debt collector is the plaintiff, and you become the defendant. You can even go to trial and meet with a lawyer to set up court-ordered payment plans based on your actual financial paperwork that you bring to the courthouse. Keep in mind that there is often interest included even after judgment is brought against you.

If you still fail to pay, a lien could be put on your property and your wages could be garnished from your current paycheck. It's legal in most states to garnish up to 25% of your wages. However, if you are seriously buried, you should know that the great state of Texas does not allow wage garnishment so if you are considering a move, Texas might be the place!

Being informed about this entire process will help you make better decisions on repairing your credit before bills go to collections. Dealing with debt collectors is its own game, so let's take a look. It's a bit different than just dealing with a credit card company. The rules have changed.

Make Debt Collectors Go Away

Unfortunately, debt collector companies just won't take your word for it that you're going through a rough time or that they need to leave you alone. They do need to see proof. Collectors love paperwork! The more proof in writing, the better. So, before calling up your debt collector to give them the complete story of why you can't pay, get yourself prepared.

Spend the time gathering up all of your financial paperwork. Get copies of your taxes that show your income and your financial situation. Gather your doctor's bills, your SSDI paperwork, your paystubs, and, if you're sharing an income or living on someone else's SSI, all the paperwork that goes along with that person.

Then, once you've gathered all your paperwork, call up your collector. Keep an eye on the prompts on the phone until you get to the customer service department. Be prepared to wait a long time on the phone. Just set aside the time to devote to this. Be polite, but brief and direct. Tell the representative that you can't pay and you have the proof you can't. Ask them how you can get them the paperwork so they can attach it to your file. Maybe you can send it in an email as a PDF attachment or mail it or fax it to them? Get the name of the representative and the state (or country) where they are. Take down your account number. Ask if you need to provide any other paperwork as proof of the inability to pay. If they tell you that you need something, comply with that. Ask if they can put a financial hardship status on your account. If so, that's great. Many collectors don't.

After you hang up, immediately follow the representative's instructions to send the paperwork to the collector. Keep all originals and only send copies. After two weeks, call up the customer service department again. Explain that you spoke to "Name" and have they received all of your paperwork? Make sure every last piece of paper is attached to your file.

The third step is to put your name on their "Do Not Call" list. VERY IMPORTANT: Keep in mind that they won't call about important stuff, either, like courtesy calls notifying you that your balance has changed. So, do this with caution. Yes, the phone calls are uber annoying. But, that's the primary legal way of contacting you.

You actually need to send your request to not be contacted in writing. Write or type legibly on a blank sheet of paper:

To Capital One,

Please put my name on your "Do Not Call" list. Please remove my name from all call lists. I understand that I will not receive any phone calls.

Thank you,

Your Name

Keep a copy, in case you need it for legal purposes. After you've mailed your request to the collector, wait three weeks for them to receive it and attach the request to your file. Your account will be flagged "Do Not Call" if it's been done properly. Follow up and call the collector to make sure your account has been flagged. Ask the representative if you need to do anything else to make sure you are not contacted.

Throughout this whole negotiating process, continue to send what payments you can. Yes, you can absolutely send small payments to a debt collector, even if it's just $10 or $20 a month. It buys you a little time to change your financial situation. Don't give up and don't just stop sending payments.

You can also settle with debt collectors. Ask them about settlement options and start with less than 50% of the debt owed. They might come back with a counter-offer. After you agree to the settlement, stick with its terms to the letter or you will be on the hook for the whole amount and you can't renegotiate for a new settlement. If you do this, make sure you have them put Paid in Full on your credit report if possible.

If your financial situation changes at any point (you get on SSI, you lose a job) or you move, then notify your debt collector immediately. Make sure the proper paperwork is attached to your file and your address is correct. You'd be surprised at how much incorrect information can get attached to your account.

WHAT IS A CREDIT REPORT AND HOW CAN I CHECK IT?

A credit report is a detailed report of your credit history. From the moment you apply for a credit card, obtain a loan, or open a utility account, the credit bureaus start collecting information on you and create a credit report based on this information. Lenders are then able to use this report, along with other information that you provide them, to determine your creditworthiness.

The Credit Bureaus

In the United States, there are three major credit bureaus: Transunion, Experian and Equifax. Each of these companies is responsible for collecting information about all consumers' including personal information, habits for paying bills and other financial data to form credit reports. Your credit report, therefore, is unique to you because you're spending habits, credit cards, loans and more will differ from other consumers. The information will be similar, but there can be some slight differences.

Breaking down Credit Reports

There is actually quite a bit of information on your credit report. First, you will notice that there is a lot of personal information such as your employment history, social security number (to differentiate you from someone with the same name), and your current and last addresses.

In addition to the personal information, the report includes a summary of your credit history. This summary contains data on the number and types of accounts you have, whether they are in good standing or past due, how high the balances are, credit limits they have and dates they were open. They are very comprehensive, but not always accurate.

The report also lists credit inquiries, and may have negative items describing some of your accounts such as collections, charge-off, judgments or liens. These items typically stay on your report for seven years unless you utilize the dispute process. Negative items impact your credit score and give a bad impression when trying to get credit.

Credit Report Access

Any time that you submit an application for credit, signs a rental agreement or obtains a new insurance policy, the creditor, landlord or insurer are legally able to access your credit report.

Employers may also request your credit report, but you need to give them permission in writing to access it. Whoever wants to obtain your credit report will need to pay the credit bureaus to access the information.

The following are those who may request access to your credit report:

- Creditors: When you apply for credit, these businesses are allowed to check your report. They can also monitor it once they have given you credit.
- Mortgage Lenders: If you are applying for a loan on a house, the mortgage lender can see some information on your credit report. If the amount borrowed is more than $150,000 they can even see some information that other creditors are not allowed to see because loan balance is so large.
- Landlords: Often times, a landlord will request access to a credit report that tracks your history of renting and whether you typically pay rent and utilities on time or have ever been evicted.
- Utility Companies: These companies are allowed to access your report, but many utility companies are regulated by the state so there could be rules against denying you services even if you have bad credit.
- Student Loan Lenders: Most students will not lose out on students if they have bad credit, but when applying for a PLUS loan, their parents may have their credit checked.
- Insurance Companies: If you are asking for a large policy, life insurance companies can see some additional older information on your credit report.

- Employers: Many employers will take a look at your credit report to evaluate if you're responsible enough for the job.
- Government Agencies: Some government agencies can use your credit report to determine if you are eligible for public assistance, can afford child support or to verify your identity.
- Collections Agencies: Collectors will sometimes look at your credit report to locate you or learn about additional assets you own.

Obtaining Your Credit Report

According to the Fair Credit Reporting Act (FCRA), the credit bureaus are required to provide consumers a copy of their credit report for free once a year. The federal law also entitles consumers to receive a credit report for free if any company takes adverse actions against them. This adverse action can include denial of employment, insurance or credit as well as notices for collections or judgments. The consumer, however, must request the report no more than 60 days from the date when the adverse action occurred. A few additional situations in which you will be able to obtain a free credit report include times when you are on welfare or unemployment and if you're a victim of identity theft.

Understanding Your Report

Generally, your credit report is divided into four parts. The first part contains all of your personal information including your social security number, name and addresses. This includes any lines of credit or other debt you currently have.

What is a good score?

Your credit score is split into several levels, but generally ranges from 300 to 850. The different credit rating levels are label as follows:

- 300 to 600: Bad Credit
- 600 to 649: Poor Credit
- 650 to 699: Fair Credit
- 700 to 749: Good Credit
- 750 + 850: Excellent Credit

The higher your credit score, the better. Better scores allow you to get credit easier, and with lower interest rates. Even when not getting credit, such as when you are renting an apartment, having a better credit rating builds trust with potential landlords.

The best thing that you can do to get your credit score up is to make payments on time. A delinquency can turn into a negative item that is much harder to remove. If you do miss payments, communicating and maintaining a good relationship with your creditor is key.

Checking my credit score

Check through your bank or your credit card issuer

This score can be found when you are logging into your online account, it is often listed in the statement segment – though may vary from companies to companies.

Buy your credit score

You can decide to buy a credit score directly from the credit reporting companies – you can decide to get it from the source itself. All you have to do is to visit the official website, set up your account, provide details of your personal information, pay the required fee and view your score.

Use a free credit score service

Many websites and platforms provide free credit score services that is designed to enlighten the borrower on the general idea of credit score. Some of these free websites offer educational scores that provide you an insight of your credit score though it may be slightly different from what a lender will see.

THE FDCPA

D ebt collecting is a multi-billion-dollar business, and there's so much misinformation out there. Creditors and borrowers are locked in a nasty struggle over paying back loans, credit cards, and credit lines. You might feel as if you're penalized no matter what you do, that companies will hike up your interest rates, reduce your credit limits, randomly change the amount of your minimum payments, or harass you with ugly phone calls at any time day or night.

But the laws around debt collecting have changed drastically in the last twenty years, due to not only the 2008 financial crisis but the collective mounting debt that Americans owe. As the borrower, you have more protection than you might think. You are not only protected by the FCRA (Fair Credit Reporting Act), but also the Truth in Lending Act and the FDCPA (Fair Debt Collection Practices Act).

The FDCPA is kind of like a borrower's bodyguard. It's a federal law that places strict limits on debt collectors who are attempting to collect your debt. Every time you're on the phone with creditors or collectors, and every time you receive a piece of mail from them, the FDCPA is working in your favor and protecting you. It seeks to find and eliminate abusive, deceptive, and unfair debt collection practices. If a debt collector harassing you is found to be in violation of the FDCPA, then you can bring a lawsuit against them and make big money, by knowing what they can't do.

Debt collectors can't mislead you, trick you, compel you, or otherwise coerce you into paying more than you owe. Go over it carefully, preferably with an attorney. Probably the biggest advantage you have as the borrower is taking debt collectors to task on how often they call you. It's considered harassment. There are specific and strict phone regulations within the FDCPA as well, that have to do with auto dialers and appropriate times to call. They can't call before 8:00 am or after 9:00 pm in your time zone. Also, if you've specifically stated that there are certain times during the day you can't be called and they do, then that is also considered harassment. Collectors cannot call your workplace unless you specifically request them to. If you have an attorney and it's on your file with them, then they can't discuss the account with you. They have to speak to your attorney.

Threats are fairly common in the debt collecting industry. Collectors will tell you that you'll get sued, you'll get arrested, your wages will be garnished, your taxes will be taken from you, you'll lose your job or your vehicle or your house, or your credit will be permanently ruined. If debt collectors use obscene, profane, or abusive language, make these threats, or in any way deal with your account in an unprofessional way, they've violated the FDCPA.

No letter, and they're in violation of the FDCPA. If they ignore your written request to verify the debt within 30 days of that notice and continue to collect on it, they have violated the FDCPA.

If any of this happens, take action immediately. All phone calls at the debt collections center are recorded. Let the collector know they are in violation of the FDCPA, you will be reporting it to an attorney, and you want a supervisor to listen to the call. If you're trying to settle the debt within a particular payment schedule or plan, you can use this as leverage. Please keep all records and paperwork to provide a nice strong case against the collector. You might be able to settle a large debt for 50% of the balance or even less, but make sure it says "paid in full" on your credit report. The language they use matters on the credit report!

You can also take it further. You can file a complaint with the FTC at their website: www.ftccomplaintassistant.gov. The FTC oversees debt collector actions. You can also file a complaint with the Consumer Financial Protection Bureau (CFPB), which passes your complaint to the creditor and works between the two of you to find a solution. To submit your complaint: www.consumerfinance.gov/complaint.

Hiring an attorney to help you fight debt collectors either in state courts or small claims courts is a great option. You still might have to pay a large amount to settle the debt, but at least you won't be continuously harassed and threatened.

FCRA AND OTHER LAWS

There is a pair of sections in the Fair Credit Reporting Act that you can use to your advantage in cleaning up your own credit report. These are the powerful secret sections of 609 and 611. Section 609 gives you the right to know what is contained within your credit report. Section 611 provides you with the means of disputing the information found in your reports.

Any information that you believe is either incorrect or unverifiable you may dispute.

The burden of proof then falls on the creditor or lender to substantiate this original debt. If they cannot do this, then you will be able to get the charges or debt taken completely off of your credit report. The Section 609 is a part of the Fair Credit Reporting Act that deals with your rights to obtain copies of your personal credit reports and related information. This section is often confused with section 611, which governs the rights to dispute a charge or debt that you owe.

Section 609 only deals with your rights to get this information that the credit bureaus have on file, not to change it.

The FCRA includes a great deal of information that gives you the ability to dispute information contained in your credit reports in this section 611. If there is information that you feel is unverifiable or incorrect, you can dispute this information.

The Federal Law and Your Credit

Not many people realize how much the federal government helps people stay protected when it comes to credit cards. On top of this, they also help you when it comes to paying back credit cards and when you find yourself in credit card debt. Sometimes, you will need to search for loopholes within the laws to help you. Other times, the law itself will help you remain protected.

Credit Card Laws

The law states you have to pay your credit card payments. If you don't, they can send your bill to collections or take you to court where the judge will order you to make payments. However, just as there are laws to protect credit card companies and ensure they get their money, there are laws to protect you.

Most of the rights for credit cardholders come from the Credit Card Act of 2009, which is also known as the credit cardholder's Bill of Rights. One of the two main areas this act helps are through transparency, which means you have to be able to understand the terms and due date. The other main area is fairness, which means they can't hike up your interest rates or cause you over-the-limit fees.

The federal law also states that you have every right to dispute a claim. In fact, credit card companies need to make sure they explain to you how to file a claim against them. They will often put up a form with directions on their website and explain it through their customer terms. At the same time, there are steps you need to follow when doing this.

First, you need to contact the number on the back of your credit card. You will then need to speak to a representative who is supposed to help solve your problem. If the problem remains unsolved or you don't feel you were treated fairly, you can then request the name, phone number, and address of the credit card company's regulatory agency. This is the agency above the credit card company that helps make sure that laws are followed and credit card companies treat their customers fairly.

The Fair Credit Billing Act states that you have the right to dispute any charge on your credit card. One of the biggest reasons you need to make sure you keep all your credit card receipts is that they will come in handy if you find something wrong with one of your transactions, whether the amount is more than you signed for or you didn't make the purchase at all. Just like filing a claim, there are certain procedures you need to follow when you are going to dispute a charge.

First, you need to send a letter to the creditor. This letter needs to be sent no later than 60 days from the transaction date. Furthermore, you need to make sure that you send a copy of the bill along with your letter. You want to make sure this is a copy and not the original bill. You need to keep both a copy of the bill and letter for your records. It doesn't matter if you are disputing a transaction or filing a claim; you want to make sure that you have copies of everything.

Second, you need to make sure that all of your information is involved in this letter. For instance, you want to not only state the amount of the transaction, but also give your name, number, and address in the letter. You can do this by placing this information at the beginning of a professional letter or at the end when you sign your name. You also want to include the date of the charge you are disputing and completely explain why you are disputing this charge. Unfortunately, an explanation such as one like you don't want the product anymore is not going to work. You need to have a reason like the company overcharged you, which the bill will show or that you didn't make the purchase.

Third, you want to make sure that the creditor has received your letter. Therefore, it is always best to send it by certified mail as this will provide you with a receipt. Of course, you can always have tracking on the letter, if this is what you prefer.

Once the creditor receives the letter, they have 30 days to send you a response in writing and 90 days to conduct an investigation. There are usually two options which conclude an investigation. The first option is you were not correct, which can mean that you owe more money. If this is the case, the company has the right to request this money within a certain amount of days. They also have the right to force you to pay any related charges. The second option is there was an error on the side of the creditor. In this case, they have to reimburse the amount and forgive any related charges.

Credit Card Act of 2009

The Credit Card Act of 2009 occurred because people were misguided about the terms that credit card companies use. They would state that they didn't understand the terms that were written and no one would explain these terms to them. After politicians listened to thousands of people reporting the same type of misguidance from credit card companies, the federal government decided to pass a law which stated credit card companies had to use more easily understood terms. After former President Obama signed the law into effect on May 22nd of 2009, credit card companies had to change their guidelines and terms so everyone could understand them ("12 consumer protections in the Credit CARD Act", n.d.).

Highlights of the Credit Card Act Of 2009

For most people, direct laws are hard to understand and often lengthy. This can cause people to briefly read the laws or give up because they simply can't understand the language. Therefore, I am going to focus on some of the highlights from the Credit Card Act of 2009.

1. You have the right to opt out

Prior to 2009, credit card customers could not opt out if the credit card company incorporated new terms customers didn't agree with. Now, you have the option to close your account as soon as you don't agree to the new terms of service. Once you close your account, you have to pay off your credit card balance within five years.

2. They are limited with raising your interest

You can't avoid the interest rakes that hike up after you purchase a card. In fact, most credit card companies will increase their interest rates annually. However, there is a limit to how much they can spike your interest rates, at least on the current amount you owe them.

In order for credit card companies to raise your interest on the amount you owe, they have to give you 45 days' notice. On top of this, they can only do it under certain conditions, such as when a promotional offer end.

3. Due dates and times need to be clear

Some credit card companies used to wait until close to your due date before they sent a monthly bill. This typically would mean that your payment would arrive late to them, which would allow them to charge you a late payment fee. The Credit Card Act of 2009 stopped this trick. Today, credit card companies have to mail your bill at least 21 days before it is due. While you might see this as a problem if you are involved with paperless billing, for many people it helps them save money.

4. Over the limit fees are now set to limits

Prior to 2009, credit card companies could charge you amount much higher than the limit fees, even if you only went a few dollars over the limit. Fortunately, they are not allowed to do this anymore. The act now states that if a customer only goes over $20, they can only charge you $20 at most, even if their over-the-limit fee is $35. This doesn't mean that credit card companies can charge you $100 if you go $100 over. At this point, they will charge you their regular fee for going over the limit.

If you have a credit card account, you have probably noticed a little bar or graph that explains to you how long it will take you to pay off your credit card if making the minimum payment. For example, it might say that if you pay the minimum, it will take you three years to pay off the total amount. They also need to state that if you want to pay off your credit card balance in 24 months, you need to pay a certain amount. These amounts are supposed to include the interest they will charge. Credit card companies have to include this knowledge due to the Credit Card Act of 2009.

5. Credit card companies can no longer target 18-year-olds

Prior to 2009, credit card companies started to target young adults. It seemed that once you turned 18, you would receive an offer from a credit card company. Of course, for many 18 and 19-year-olds, this is exciting because it was supposed to help them pay for their college textbooks or buy groceries. Unfortunately, this caused a lot of college students to fall into credit card debt quickly. Today, credit card companies can no longer approve of anyone who is not 21 years of age.

It is important to mention that there are exceptions when it comes to this. Credit card companies can approve someone between the ages of 18 and 20 if they have a co-signer who is over 21 and have proof of income that will allow them to make regular monthly payments. Another important notice of this part of the Credit Card Act of 2009 is that credit card companies can no longer offer free rewards for applying for a credit card if they are within 1,000 feet of a university campus.

One thing to remember when it comes to credit card and federal regulations is they can change every year. Therefore, it is important to take your time to make sure you are updated on the laws surrounding credit cards, your credit card debt, and your rights as a cardholder.

REBUILD YOUR CREDIT

Credit card debts are probably seen as something that cause great distress. The good news is that you can break free from the bondage of debt. Apart from rebuilding your credit history, your mentality should be focused on getting out of debt and building wealth. Dumping debt is empowering. And you have the power to stay out of debt if you really want to.

The following are added information on how you can rebuild your credit and finally proclaim yourself, debt free.

Use Good Credit to Leverage Your Way Up

If you have gone through a bad experience about credit cards, you would probably associate the word "credit" with the word "bad". Good credit breeds good credit. Part of the technique is to use your credit and be wise enough to become a person of good standing. With a good credit rating, you are able to get the best interest rates on your loans and credit cards. Having good credit standing helps you become more aware of your status and keep to it. Collection calls are now a thing of the past. The constant feeling of worrying how to settle your monthly dues are no longer a major concern. Bills are paid off and you feel a certain kind of control, freedom, and peace of mind.

There Needs to Be an Activity and Constant Update

In order to rebuild your credit, do not let old information sit for a long time. Your credit report should always have recent activities listed for at least six months. Be active and generate good information. There has to be timely and consistent pattern of payments so you can be flagged for consistent payments. Having regular activity means your credit report gets fresh update on a monthly basis.

Get a Secured Credit Card

This is another way to prove that you are credit worthy. If getting a regular credit card is not possible, you may get a secured card. It works in a way that you deposit a certain amount in the bank, and in essence, allow you to borrow it back. Your credit limit depends on the money that you have deposited. Pay your monthly fees on time and request for a regular card after a year of no delay payments. Finally, the more important part is that you confirm with the credit union if they turn in your good standing information to the credit reporting agencies. Remember your purpose in getting the card – build your credit rating. So if they are not going to turn up on the credit report, this whole thing of rebuilding your credit is pointless.

Borrow a Small Installment Loan from Your Trusted Bank

This is another way towards a stellar credit report. It may seem odd at first but know that credit scores are calculated based on having different kinds of loans and not just credit cards. You can just opt to borrow a small amount from the bank and keep the length of the loan for at least a year. The goal is to establish a new credit path and have regular activity to spark your credit score.

Co-Sign a Loan with Someone

Just a word of caution: co-sign a loan with someone whom you know is responsible enough to take on debt and pay for it. Remember, when you co-sign, you share the debt. And, if they fail to repay the debt, the lending bank will come to you for full payment. Also, if your spouse or a family member is an authorized user of your credit card, you can make him/her a joint account holder. Getting credit under each person's name can give you good credit.

Completely Eliminate Your Debt for Life

If there is one method that would cure your debts and worries away that would have to be debt elimination. You can do this by allotting money meant for your bills. Or, if you have saved up for the rainy days, now is the time to take that out and lessen your debts. Paying them could save you with hundreds and thousands of dollars on interest rates. You would not want to pay high interest rates for life, don't you?

Apply the Debt Reduction Method

All you have to do is prepare a simple draft of your income statement showing your net worth, a balance sheet, and two letters from your CPA. Showing concrete statements is one of your most powerful tools in reducing your debt drastically. Just do not forget to consult your financial adviser about this.

Always Check for Identity Theft

There is a high probability that there could be an unexplained item (s) in your credit report that does not belong to you. Sad fact is that it is a bad credit score. If this happens, you could be denied credit and you are going to pay for it. So if there is something mysterious that you see in your credit report, call the credit card company immediately. You need to act fast because you could be a victim of identity theft. It is a real threat.

Avoid becoming a victim by following these safety tips:

- Do not disclose any personal information over the phone such as your social security number and credit card number.
- Almost all thefts occur online, so be smart when doing your online banking. Always log off your account once finished.
- Do not download anything that pops up on your computer.
- Change your password regularly.
- Run an antivirus or security software all the time.

- Do not use online banking when on a Wi-Fi network at public places.

Be Wiser When Handling Finances

You have probably learned your lesson the hard way. But what is important is that you learn from it and act on it. This way, you will not fall victim of this scrupulous scheme again and somehow learn how to play this tricky game.

CREDIT BUREAUS

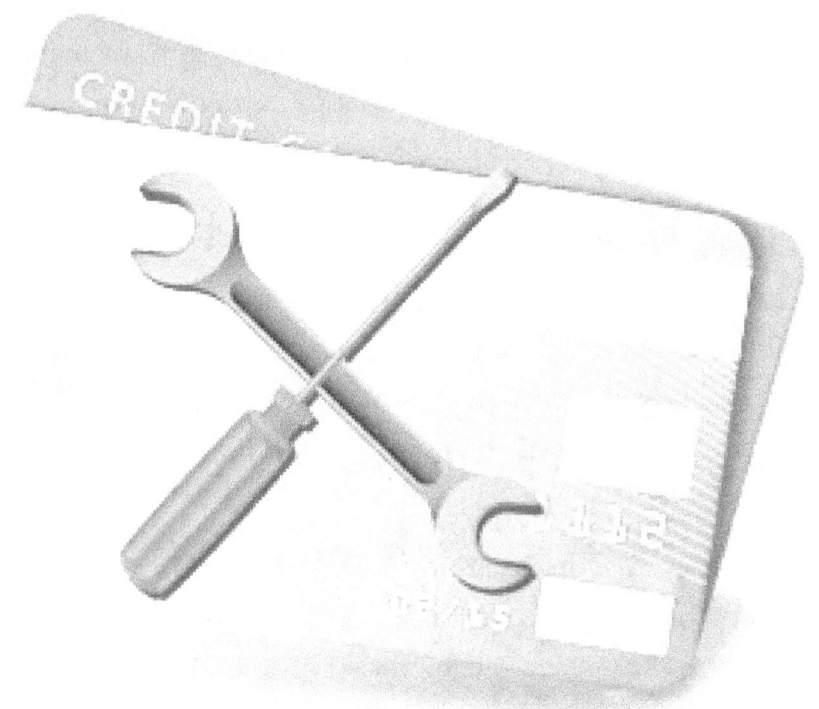

Credit bureaus are privately held, billion-dollar organizations whose primary reason for existing is to make cash; that is what revenue driven organizations do right? They keep data that lenders furnish them - regardless of whether accurate or inaccurate - about our credit association with them and sell it. This straightforward plan of action generates over $4 Billion per year!

One wellspring of income for them originates from selling the information on our credit reports to different lenders, managers, insurance agencies, credit card organizations - and whoever else you approve to see your credit information. In addition to the fact that they provide them with crude data; yet they likewise sell them various methods for examining the data to decide the risk of stretching out credit to us. In addition to trading our information to lenders, they likewise sell our information to us - credit scores, credit observing administrations, extortion security, wholesale fraud prevention - interestingly enough this region has quickly gotten perhaps the greatest wellspring of income. Furthermore, those pre-endorsed offers in our letter drop each week; or garbage mail? That's right; they got our information from the credit bureaus as well. Organizations buy in to an assistance provided by the three credit bureaus that sell them a rundown of consumer's credit information that fit a pre-decided criterion.

Presently, as opposed to prevalent thinking, credit bureaus don't have any contribution on whether you ought to be endorsed for a loan or not; that is absolutely based on the credit criteria of the lender you're working with. However, by utilizing the entirety of the information that has been set on your credit report (personal information, payment history, and credit propensities) and FICO's technique for scoring that data, they do tell them with how creditworthy you are.

Origin and History of Credit Bureau

In recent decades, credit has gotten easier and easier to obtain. Credit cards, for example, were once given to the wealthier classes in the public eye and were utilized just occasionally. Toward the start of the twenty-first century, practically 50% of all Americans had in any event one broadly useful credit card (that is, a Visa, MasterCard, American Express, or Discover card). The ascent of credit as a typical method to buy necessities, extravagances, and everything in the middle of implies that credit bureaus process more information and are a more crucial part of the general economy than any other time in recent memory. Credit bureaus likewise monitor and investigate the data got from a regularly expanding number of loans for homes, cars, and other high-cost things.

Today, credit bureaus consistently accumulate information from creditors (banks; credit-card guarantors; mortgage organizations, which have practical experience in loaning cash to home buyers; and different businesses that stretch out credit to people and businesses) and amass it into files on singular consumers and businesses, while refreshing their current files. In addition to the data gathered from creditors, credit files may likewise contain one's business history, previous addresses, false names, bankruptcy filings, and removals. Information usually remains on a credit report for seven years before being evacuated.

The greater part of the nearby and provincial consumer credit bureaus in the United States are claimed by or are under agreement to one of the three essential consumer credit-reporting administrations referenced previously. Every one of these three organizations assembles and appropriates information separately, and credit scores and reports vary somewhat from bureau to bureau. Each organization keeps up around 200 million singular consumer credit files. Frequently a lender will utilize an average of the credit evaluations provided by the three unique bureaus when choosing whether to make a loan.

The basic business credit bureau in the United States is Dun and Bradstreet. D and B have credit files on more than 23 million associations in North America and on more than 100 million businesses around the globe. In addition to giving creditors information important to decide a credit applicant's capabilities, credit bureaus make their data accessible for progressively questionable purposes. For example, standard mail advertisers regularly buy information from credit bureaus as they continued looking for potential clients. If that you have ever gotten a letter revealing to you that you have been pre-endorsed for a particular credit card at a particular yearly percentage rate, it is valid; the credit-card organization definitely realizes your credit rating and has to be sure previously affirmed you for the predefined card. Forthcoming managers and proprietors sometimes buy credit histories, as well.

What Credit Bureaus Do?

Credit bureaus collect information from various sources in accordance with consumer information. The activity is done for various reasons and includes data from singular consumers. Included is the information concerning a people charge payments and their getting. Utilized for evaluating creditworthiness, the information provides lenders with an outline of your accounts if a loan repayment is required. The interest rates charged on a loan are additionally worked out concerning the kind of credit score shown by your experience. It is thusly not a uniform procedure, and your credit report is the significant instrument that affects future loans.

Based on risk based valuing, it pegs various risks on the various customers in this manner deciding the cost you will acquire as a borrower. Done as credit rating, it is an assistance provided to various interested parties in the public. Terrible credit histories are affected for the most part by settled court commitments that mark you for high interest rates every year. Duty liens and bankruptcies, for example, shut you out of the conventional credit lines and may require a great deal of arrangement for any loan to be offered by the bank.

Bureaus collect and examine credit information including financial data, personal information, and elective data. This is given by various sources generally marked data furnishers. These have an exceptional association with the credit bureaus. An average gathering of data furnishers would comprise of creditors, lenders, utilities, and debt collection agencies. Any association that has had payment involvement in the consumer is qualified including courts. Any data collected for this situation is provided to the credit bureaus for grouping. When it is accumulated, the data is placed into specific repositories and files claimed by the bureau. The information is made accessible to customers upon request. The idea of such information is important to lenders and managers.

The information is in this manner material in various conditions; credit evaluation and business thought are simply part of these. The consumer may likewise require the information to check their individual score and the home proprietor may need to check their inhabitants report before renting an apartment. Since borrowers saturate the market, the scores will, in general, be robotic. Straightforward examination would deal with this by giving the client a calculation for speedy appraisal. Checking your score once every other year should deal with errors in your report.

Individuals from the public are qualified for one free credit report from every one of the significant bureaus. Business reports, for example, Paydex might be gotten to on request and are chargeable. Lawful expressions for the credit bureaus incorporate credit report agency, CRA in the US. This is organized in the Fair Credit Report Act, FCTA. Other government rules associated with the assurance of the consumer incorporate Fair and Accurate Credit Transaction Act, Fair Credit Billing Act and Regulation B. Statutory bodies have additionally been made for the regulation of the credit bureaus. The Fair Trade Commission serves to as a controller for the consumer credit report agencies while the Office of the Comptroller of Currency fills in as a manager of all banks going about as furnishers.

TRANSUNION, EQUIFAX AND EXPERIAN

Three Major Credit Bureaus

The popular credit bureaus have a significant effect on every consumer, but many people don't know these companies or how they work.

- Experian
- Equifax
- Trans Union

The ideal approach to manage your credit capably and assume responsibility for your financial circumstance is to be educated. This takes a brief period and exertion on your part, yet since your credit scores are so important to dealing with your accounts and setting aside cash, it's your duty to know as much as you can regard the credit bureaus that formulate credit appraisals. To assist you with getting a running beginning on that strategy, some information on Transunion, Experian and Equifax, the primary credit bureaus in the U.S.:

Transunion

Transunion has workplaces the nation over that manages various parts of credit: credit management, identity theft, and other credit issues; and types of credit customers, for example, personal, business, and press inquiries. If you discover errors on your Transunion credit report, you can call them at 800.916.8800 or visit their site to debate them. If that you believe that you're a casualty of identity theft, call them at 800.680.7289 at the earliest opportunity.

Experian

Like other credit bureaus, Experian provides a wide range of various administrations for people, businesses, and the media Rather, they encourage guests to utilize online forms for questions, identity theft reports, and different issues.

Equifax

Based in Atlanta, GA, Equifax likewise has various departments to help people with various types of questions and concerns. Their website is additionally set up to have people utilized online forms to address errors, report identity theft, and handle different concerns. In any case, if somebody believes that their identity has been taken, the individual in question can, however, call 888.397.3742 to report it to Equifax. If that somebody detects a blunder on their Equifax credit report, that person must utilize the contact number on the report to question it. There is no number on the site to describe errors.

These are the 3 credit bureaus in the nation, and they each adopt an alternate strategy to enabling people to get in touch with them to pose inquiries or address any issues they might be encountering. Rather than reaching the credit bureaus legitimately, numerous people prefer to utilize a credit checking administration to assist them with dealing with their credit and stay over their funds. The credit bureaus all have comparative projects; however, most people prefer to utilize a free organization to assist them with these issues. That way, they get an impartial perspective on their credit score and a lot more devices to proactively manage and improve their credit ratings.

These companies have a great history in the financial industry. Also known as a credit reporting agency, it gathers financial information about consumers and combines this information into a single report. Since these bureaus work independently, the credit report that a single bureau generates for an individual could be slightly different from another bureau's report. Although there are smaller credit bureaus, the top three serve a more significant share of the market.

The credit bureaus have a fascinating profit model. Lenders, banks, and many other companies share a lot of information about their clients with credit bureaus for free. The credit bureaus process this information and put it on sale, in the form of a credit report, to different parties that require insight into your financial history, and more.

Thinking about just one number to represent your credit score is a little too simple. You actually have multiple credit scores, each calculated and maintained by a different company. Usually these scores are very close to each other, but they almost always vary by at least a few points.

The three bureaus are Equifax, Experian, and Transunion. We will get into the reason that the scores are different a little bit later, but it has to do with the way they collect information. Your score from any of these three companies will be called your FICO.../../Downloads/h - _ftn1 score (it may also be a

BEACON score from Equifax). If it is called something different, it is just an estimate, and is not the real deal. As we will find out later, that may be ok in some cases, but it is something you should be aware of.

In addition to the three companies, each one actually keeps up to 7 different scores per person. For our purposes, we are just going to focus on what is called the classic or generic score. So from here on out, the words "score" or "credit score" mean the classic or generic score. It is the most commonly used for most purposes (buying a house or getting a loan), and the other scores will follow it up or down for the most part. We aren't worried about two or three points here; we are looking for the biggest changes we can make with the least effort.

Dealing with Credit Bureaus

Today, where the economy is at its weak point, having a good credit is a necessary tool. This is because it allows you to obtain house loans, car loans, credit card, and other convenient financial services and instruments. You may be able to live without having a good credit.

You can discern the credit bureau that holds your file by looking at any rejection letter you received from a recent credit application.

If you are dealing with the credit bureau that handles your file, keep in mind that it belongs in the business of collecting and selling information. As such, you should not provide them with any detail, which is not necessary legally.

When you already have your credit report, make sure to check for any error or discrepancy. If you find anything that is questionable in your report, you can send the credit bureau a written request for them to investigate on the error. In general, the credit bureau has the burden of documenting anything that is included in your credit report. If the credit bureau fails to investigate on the error or neglects your request for an investigation within 30 days, the error should be removed.

You need to educate yourself about the legal obligations of credit bureaus in order to have a successful credit repair process. Prior to dealing with them, make sure you know all the legal aspects so you would not end up paying for something that should not be charged with a fee. Remember, credit bureaus are also businesses and that they own many credit repairs companies.

Making the Best of Credit Bureaus

It is a little annoying to learn that all three credit bureaus have sensitive financial data. However, there's no method to prevent lenders and collection entities from sharing your information with the above companies.

You can limit any possible problems associated with the credit bureaus by evaluating your credit reports annually, and acting immediately in case, you notice some errors. It is also good to monitor your credit cards and other open credit products to ensure that no one is misusing the accounts. If you have a card that you don't often use, sign up for alerts on that card so that you get notified if any transactions happen, and regularly review statements for your active cards. Next, if you notice any signs of fraud or theft, you can choose to place a credit freeze with the three credit bureaus and be diligent in tracking the activity of your credit card in the future.

How the Bureaus Get Their Information

To learn how the score is calculated, first we need to learn about all the different inputs of your score, aka where the bureaus get their info. You may have many factors that report information to the credit bureaus, or none.

Credit cards are called revolving accounts or revolving debt by the credit bureaus. Each monthly payment and balance is reported, as well as any late payments. This means that any cards that have your name on them will also report to all the bureaus. This includes cards that belong to a spouse or parent. If you're an authorized user on the account it gets reported on your credit no matter what. Many people have their credit ruined by a spouse or parent going into bankruptcy or not paying their credit card bills. If your name is on any credit cards that belong to people that may not pay their bills, ask them to take your name off immediately!

Installment loans also report information to the credit bureaus. If you went down to your local Sears and financed a washer/dryer set by putting up a down payment, that is an installment loan. The details of these loans are all reported; the total balance, as well as the timeliness and amounts of your monthly payments.

If you have mortgages or student loans, that information does get reported. Total amounts due, total paid so far, and the status of monthly payments is all reported. This information is all kept track of and organized in their databases.

SECTION 609

Basically, a 609 is known as a dispute letter, which you would send to your creditor if you saw you were overcharged or unfairly charged. Most people use a 609 letter in order to get the information they feel they should have received. There are several reasons why some information might be kept from you.

A section 609 letter is sent after two main steps. First, you see that the dispute is on your credit report. Second, you have already filed and processed a debt validation letter. The basis of the letter is that you will use it in order to take unfair charges off of your credit report, which will then increase your credit score.

The 609 letters can easily help you delete your bad credit. Other than this, there are a couple of other benefits you will receive from the letter. One of these benefits is that you will obtain your documentation and information as the credit bureau has to release this information to you. Secondly, you will be able to obtain an accurate credit report, which can definitely help you increase your credit score.

There are also disadvantages to the 609 letters. One of these disadvantages is that collection agencies can add information to your credit history at any time. A second disadvantage is that you still have to repay debt. You cannot use the 609 letters in order to remove debt that you are obligated to pay. Finally, your creditor can do their own investigation and add the information back into your credit report, even if it was removed (Irby, 2019).

One of the reasons section 609 came to be is because one of five people state they have inaccurate information on the credit report (Black, 2019). At the same time many people believe that this statistic is actually higher than 20 percent of Americans.

How Section 609 Works to Repair Bad Credit

If you notice anything on your report that should not be there, you need to use the section 609 loophole in order to file a dispute, which could result in their wrong information being taken off of the report.

How to File a Dispute with Section 609

What this means is that you can easily download and use one of these templates yourself. While you usually have to pay for them, there are some which are free. Of course, you will want to remember to include your information in the letter before you send it.

You will want to make sure everything is done correctly as this will make it more likely that the information will come off and no one will place it back on your report again.

1. Find a dispute letter through goggling "section 609 dispute letter".

2. Make the necessary changes to the letter. This will include changing the name and address. You will also want to make sure your phone number is included. Sometimes people include

their email address, but this is not necessary. In fact, it is always safer to only include your home address or PO Box information. You will also want to make sure to edit the whole letter. If something does not match up to what you want to say in your letter, such as what you are trying to dispute on your credit report, you need to state this. These letters are quite generic, which means you need to add in your own information.

3. You also want to make sure you use blue ink rather than black. On top of this, you do not need to worry about being too neat, but you want to make sure they can read the letters and numbers correctly. This is an important part of filing your dispute letter because handwritten ones in blue ink will not be pushed through their automated system. They have an automatic system which will read the letter for them and punch in the account number you use. They will then send you a generic letter that states these accounts are now off your credit report, which does not mean that it actually happened. When you write the information down, a person needs to read it and will typically take care of it. Of course, this does not mean that you will not be pushed aside. Unfortunately, this can happen with any letters.

4. You want to make sure that you prove who you are with your letters. While this is never a comfortable thing to do, you must send a copy of your social security card and your driver's license or they will shred your letter. You can typically do this by visiting your county's courthouse.

5. You can send as many letters as you need to; however, keep in mind that the creditor typically will not make you send more than four. This is because when you threaten to take them to court in the third letter, they will realize that your accounts and demands just are not worth it. First, you could damage their reputation, and secondly, you will cost them more money than simply taking the information off of your credit report will.

6. You will want to make sure that you keep all correspondence they send you. This will come in handy when they try to make you send more information or keep telling you that they cannot do anything. Many people struggle to get them to pay attention because that is just how the system works. Therefore, you need to make sure that you do not listen to their quick automatic reply that your information is off of your credit report. You also want to make sure to wait at least three months and then re-run your credit report to make sure the wrong information has been removed. Keep track of every time you need to re-run your credit report as you can use this as proof if they continue to send you a letter stating the information is off of your credit report.

It is important to note that you can now file a dispute letter online with all three credit bureaus. However, this is a new system, which means that it does come with more problems than sending one through the mail. While it is completely your choice whether you use a form to file your 609 dispute or send a letter, you always want to make sure you keep copies and continue to track them, even if you don't hear from the credit bureau after a couple of months. It will never hurt to send them a second letter or even a third.

What Are My Rights Under 609?

The Fair Credit Reporting Act is going to cover a lot of the aspects and the components of credit checking to make sure that it is able to maintain a reasonable amount of privacy and accuracy along the way. This agency is going to list all of the responsibilities that credit reporting companies and any credit bureaus will have, and it also includes the rights of the consumer which will be your rights in this situation. This Act is going to be the part that will govern how everything is going to work to ensure that all parties are treated in a fair manner.

When using this act the consumer has to be told if any of the information that is on your file has been in the past or is now being used against you in any way, shape, or form. You have a right to know whether the information is harming you and what that information is.

In addition, the consumer is going to have the right to go through and dispute any information that may be seen as inaccurate or incomplete at the time. If they see that there are items in the documents they are sent, if the billing to them is not right or there is something else off in the process, the consumer has the right to dispute this and the credit reporting agency needs to at least look into it and determine if the consumer is right.

This Act is going to limit the access that third parties can have to your file. You personally have to go through and provide your consent before someone is able to go through and look at your credit score, whether it is a potential employer or another institution providing you with funding.

They are not able to get in and just look at it. Keep in mind that if you do not agree for them to take a look at the information, it is going to likely result in you not getting the funding that you want, because there are very few ways that the institution can fairly assess the risk that you pose to them in terms of creditworthiness.

It means that you may have debt or another negative item that is on your credit report, but there is a way to get around this without having to wait for years to get that to drop off your report or having to pay back a debt that you are not able to afford.

Keep in mind that this is not meant to be a method for you to take on a lot of debts that you cannot afford and then just dump them. But on occasion, there could be a few that you are able to fight and get an instant boost to your credit score in the process.

Why Use a 609 Letter?

The 609 Letter is going to be one of the newest credit repair secrets that will help you to remove a lot of information on your credit report, all of the false information and sometimes even the accurate information, thanks to a little loophole that is found in our credit reporting laws. You can use this kind of letter in order to resolve some of the inaccuracies that show up, to dispute your errors, and handle some of the other items that could inaccurately come in and impact and lower your credit score.

Using these 609 letters is a good way for us to clean up our credit a bit and in some cases, it is going to make a perfect situation. However, we have to remember that outside of some of the obvious benefits that we are going to discuss, there are a few things that we need to be aware of ahead of time.

There are few limitations that are going to come with this as well, for example, even after you work with the 609 letters, it is possible that information that is seen as accurate could be added to the report again, even after the removal. This is going to happen if the creditor is able to verify the accuracy. They may take it off for a bit if the 30 days have passed and they are not able to verify at that point. But if the information is accurate, remember that it could end up back on the report.

HOW TO WRITE A CREDIT REPAIR LETTER 609

Writing the Dispute Letter

Removing adverse information from your credit report is the most vital step when trying to improve your score on a short-term basis.

Credit reporting agencies (CRAs) are not obligated to give notification when adverse information is being reported about you. Upon receiving your information, the CRAs' only job under the law is to use their "reasonable procedures" to validate accuracy.

However, there is no proper and detailed explanation of these procedures, like a list of what must be performed. Of course, if the CRAs were legally required to corroborate every piece of information they receive, they will burn out and shut down.

The Disputing Process

The first thing you need to know is that all three credit reporting agencies have to contest the inaccurate information independently. The disputed appearance may be on all three credit reports, or may not. Keep in mind that customers may not belong to all credit reporting agencies. This is why you will see that on one list some of the investors are not on the others.

Even though all three credit reporting agencies have the same information, this does not mean that if an item comes out of one credit report it will come out of the others. No promise is provided what the outcome will be. That is why you have to refute any inaccurate information about each particular article.

They can use their appeal forms when disputing with credit reporting agencies, write your own message, or challenge the item online on their Website. If you decide to dispute by letter writing, simply state the facts in a simple, concise or two sentences.

If you've found more than four entries on your credit report that you need to dispute, don't dispute everything in one letter. Whether you're writing a letter, filling out their form or answering via the Internet, break your disputes. You send or go back every 30 days to the website of the credit reporting agency, and challenge up to four more things. Don't overshoot that number. If you have to challenge less than four things, go ahead and dispute the remaining entries. Extend the spacing of conflicts for 30 days.

On submitting each address, expect to receive a revised credit report about 45 days after you send your letter or disagreement online. If your new credit report has not been issued before it's time to appeal the second time, go ahead and mail your second letter or challenge online instead.

Once all the grievance letters have been mailed or posted to their website and all the revised credit reports have been received, check whether products have been omitted or incomplete. If you need to do the procedure again for the remaining items, space 120 days from your most recent update to the next round of disputes.

CRAs Verification Forms

The FCRA tries to balance the game for consumers with the dispute process.

The dispute process gave the CRAs so much work, so they opted to restructure their dispute process—so they designed and provided a dispute form for consumers and separate verification forms for their source creditors.

Unsurprisingly, completing and returning verification forms are easier for creditors. Moreover, because the CRAs have 30 days to answer to your dispute, either to verify or correct an item, creditors are given a few weeks to return the CRAs the verification forms. However, bear something in mind: not every source creditor will turn around these forms within the allotted period—some will not even return it, at all. Just because of this, several disputes will bring about items being corrected or deleted.

Fill-In Dispute Forms

Below is an example of a multiple choice dispute options:

- The account/item is not mine.
- The account status is incorrect.
- The account/item is too old to be included in my report.

When trying to initiate a dispute using the online platform, a pop-up may come to ask you if you want to dispute an item. Just select "yes" to continue.

This is just a protection clause used by the CRAs to trick you into thinking that it is illegal to dispute an item the CRAs consider as valid or correct.

Scale through their scare tactic and do not be intimidated. Just know that it is under the law for you to dispute any inaccurate information or item.

If you requested for your reports to be sent via email, among the documents will be a dispute form. The CRAs will advise to fill this already typed form only if there are any inaccuracies on your report. The funny thing is that these mailed dispute forms are simpler to complete because of two reasons:

1. Broadcasting their conformity to the legally required dispute process gives them more acclaim.
2. Supplying their forms is more convenient for them— because, with these simplified forms, their trained agents can swiftly read and convey the information on to their creditor verification forms.

If you have simple disputes (listed in a box or a line on the form), you can either use the online or mailed disputes forms. However, if your issues are complex or lengthy and cannot fit into the allotted space or there are not enough options on the document to address all your dispute issues, you may need to write the CRAs.

Concerning the mailed fill-in dispute forms, be cautious when filling them out as they may ask you to give out more personal information to the CRAs than you need to. The CRAs asking for more information does not mean you have to provide it. Just remember that if a fill-in dispute form does not adequately help your case, the best course of action is to write your letter.

How to Write Your Own Dispute Letter

After organizing all your items, you can write your letter, but make sure to put your disputes in one correspondence. It does not matter if you have a long list of disputes. You can arrange your disputes on multiple pages and in different ways.

For instance, in the left column, list all your accounts; in the right column, list the issues in a few words ("not my account," "always paid on time/never late," etc.). Alternatively, you explain your dispute first, then list the accounts associated with the issue. For example, "the following accounts do not belong to me. . ." Just keep it short and straightforward.

When disputing an item with the bureaus you want to be sure that you have a valid reason and are requesting the correct items to be investigated.

Making sure that you are air tight in your dispute reasoning is important.

You will find that dispute reasons will add validity to your future disputes. If you choose to hire an attorney to pursue legal actions, the letters submitted may be called to be used in court.

Do yourself a favor and make sure you are using real dispute instructions with real reasoning behind them. What is meant by this is that you want to make sure that if you are disputing an account and you do not have solid proof that it is reporting inaccurately or in error then leave some room to be wrong. If you come out and say - THIS ACCOUNT ISNT MINE, then you is lying and are committing fraud (don't do that).

Sending Your Dispute Letter

When correcting information on your credit report, make sure it reflects with all three CRAs. Even when one or two reports do not show an error appearing on the other, be on the safe side by telling all of them about the error. Do it because the error might be a recent one and has yet to spread to other reports.

Even if you have not received all three reports, send a dispute letter to all three CRAs. Know that you are a consumer, so an error on one report could mean the same error is on other reports. It is not crime disputing with all CRAs. Of course, if you can start the dispute process with one CRA, you will not have much trouble doing with the others. When a CRA cannot find an error, it will respond with a letter informing you about it.

Whether you are using the CRA dispute form or drafting your dispute letter, use only certified mail with return receipt requested. While a CRA hardly claims not to have received your letter, sending certified mail is still best for your correspondence, especially in cases of pressing legal disputes like identity theft.

Call the CRA to know whether your dispute was received. Note that when talking with CRA agents, be careful not to give them the information you do not want to be included on your report.

The following is a list of CRA customer service phone numbers:

- Equifax: (800) 685-1111
- Experian: (888) 397-3742
- Transunion: (800) 916-8800

As soon as a CRA gets your dispute letter, it notifies you, and then informs you later of the completion of the verification process. You may get a response much sooner than 30 days—it all depends on the number of accounts you are disputing and the speed of at which source creditors give back the verification forms. Still, give it up to 40 days. If you do not get anything after 40 days, know that your dispute was not recognized, so send another one.

What Is Found in A CRA's Response to a Dispute?

After receiving your corrected reports, carefully read through them. The first or second page should include a paragraph stating the information reinvestigated upon your request, next is a list of affected accounts and the results of the reinvestigation. Here you will see one or more of the three possible outcomes regarding the dispute process:

1. Deleted: Deleted accounts—like they never existed.
2. Verified—No Change: No changes were made. The accounts will continue to report information
3. Update: This could mean one of three things:
    a. Deleted late or past due indications.
    b. After the review of the account by the source creditor, a small adjustment was made, and it does not affect your report.

c. Along with the forms, the source creditor returns an updated submission on your file (a requirement after every few months) to update your account. In this case, do not be fooled by the "update" notification, and make sure the first issue has been addressed. If not, send a follow-up letter.

Make Sure Everything Is Readable

No matter what you send, you want to make sure that someone else will be able to read it. This is another reason why having someone proofread your letter is often the best option as they will be able to tell you if something isn't readable or doesn't make sense.

While you should do your best to type as much information as possible, you shouldn't write the letter by hand. While this will be accepted, it is generally not something that people do in this day and age. Furthermore, typing most of the information will ensure that words are not mistaken for another word, which can happen with handwriting. While you might feel your handwriting is easily readable, someone else might not be able to understand it as well.

GOODWILL LETTERS

Goodwill letters are not a guaranteed method of removing negative information from your credit report but are still worth a try in some situations. They are more effective if you have a good history with the company, have had a technical error delayed your payment, or if your autopay did not go through. You can sometimes even convince a credit company to forgive a late payment if you simply forgot to pay.

Try to contact your credit agency by phone to negotiate and explain your situation before sending a goodwill letter. This tactic might be all that you need to do in order to remove the record of the late payment. The sooner you contact, the better as well. If you notice that you have a late payment, calling right away could stop it from being reported at all.

To write a goodwill letter you should:

- Use courteous language that reflects your remorse for the late payment and thank the company for their service.
- Include reasons you need to have the record removed such as qualifying for a home or auto loan or insurance.
- Accept that you were at fault for the late payment.
- Explain what caused the payment to be made late.

To write a goodwill letter you should not:

o Be forceful, rude, or flippant about the situation.

Goodwill Letter Template

Date

Your Name

Your Address

Your City, State, Zip Code

Name of Credit Company

Address

City, State, Zip Code

Re: Account Number

Dear Sir or Madame,

Thank you [company's name] for continued service. I am writing in regard to an urgent request concerning a tradeline on my credit reports that I would like to have reconsidered. I have taken pride in making my payments on time and in full since I received [name of credit line/card] on [date that you received the credit]. Unfortunately, I was unable to pay on time [date of missed payment(s)] due to [detailed and personal reason for not being able to pay on time. You might want to include several sentences using as much information as possible to plead your case.]

[Follow up your reason for not paying on time with a concession of guilt such as:] I have come to see that despite [reason listed above], I should have been better prepared/more responsible with my finances to ensure the payment was on time. I have worked on [some type of learning or way of improving your situation] in order to prevent this situation from happening again.

I am in need of/about to apply for [new credit line such as a home loan] and it has come to my attention that the notation on my credit report of [credit company's] late payment may prevent me from qualifying or receiving the best interest rates. Due to the fact that this notation is not a reflection of my status with [Credit Company], I am requesting that you please give me another chance at a positive credit rating by revising my tradelines.

If you need any additional documentation or information from me in order to reach a positive outcome, please feel free to contact me.

Thank you again for your time,

Sincerely yours,

Your Name

Signature

THE RIGHT MINDSET

Many folks suffer a financial crisis at some point. They may have to deal with overspending, loss of a job, a family member or personal illness. These financial problems can be and usually are, overwhelming. To make these situations worse, most people don't even know where to begin to solve these financial dilemmas. Our goal here is to shine some light on the strategies to help get youth Accumulating basic consumer debt will chain you into slavery and you could possibly spend your life held down by your own obligations to repay these loans. Who do you work for? I don't care what you say; the real answer is your creditors if you are currently stuck paying debt. There are many forms of "dumb debt" you can get trapped into. We are all sold images and lifestyles hundreds of times per day to provoke this materialistic behavior.

The person or institution lending you the money is trusting that you have the ability to hold up your end of the bargain, basically. Sometimes, it may seem impossible to live your life without the option to get a credit, but this is what bad credit eventually leads to.

But how do you get a credit in the first place? What is the process you have to go through to loan money? Well, it all starts with a credit application to a bank or some other party that has the necessary finances. Your application is reviewed and, if they think there won't be a problem with getting their money back, you sign a contract and get your money in no time. The application you submit to a lender is used to obtain a credit report from one or several reporting agencies, depending on how much money you need. These two documents are given scores and, if your score is enough, you'll get the money you need. The more "good credit" criteria you meet, the more likely it is that you will get your credit.

However, there are several things that you must consider before you put yourself into the category of citizens unaffected by bad credit. First of all, the lenders look for certain things in your application, such as an up to date credit report and no late payments on your other financial obligations. They are interested to see if you've had a job for more than a year and have a stable income, as well as a stable residence. They also evaluate the situation of your utility and phone bills and appreciate if you include information about additional credit cards or other types of cards. It is not only banks and money lenders that look at this type of information. Sometimes, if you want to get a new job, your employer will conduct this type of research too, so maintaining a good credit is crucial in these troubled times we live in.

What type of credit should you get, the most used types of credit are secured and signature credits. For smaller loans, there's no need for that, as no institution would like to end up with a store of household items, so they lend you money or issue a credit card in your name simply based on the strength of your credit so far.

There is hope; you as the borrower have many options to get rid of debt. You can take advantage of budgeting and other techniques, such as debt consolidation, debt settlement, credit counseling, and bankruptcy procedures. You just have to choose the best strategy that will work for you. When choosing from the various options, you have to consider your debt level, your discipline, and plans for the future.

The Good Debt

Some people find it hard to live debt free at least they will have some debt to pay off. While some debts are discouraged, good debt is considered as the money you borrow so that you can pay for things that you really need or things that increase in value. On the flip side, bad debt is one that arises from things that you only want and often decrease in value.

Of course, debt isn't a bad thing; it's just how you use the money that matters.

For a good debt, you will always have a good reason to justify it, and a developed plan for paying it so that you can clear the debt as quickly as possible.

An individual with good debt will also have the cheapest methods of borrowing money. They will do this by looking at the borrowing method, rate of interest, credit amount, and charges that are appropriate to them.

Sometimes, it may imply a deal with the least possible interest rate, but sometimes, it may not.

Examples of good debt

Paying for medical care. There is no fixed amount of money to borrow to ensure your loved one stays healthy. You can manage to pay off the money you borrow, but it is impossible to replace a human life. If a person requires expensive treatments to ensure they remain healthy, this would be an acceptable debt, no matter what.

Borrow money for education. When you apply for a student loan debt, you aren't making a wrong decision. And applying for a student loan so that you can support the education of your child defeats the idea of using your savings. After all, you cannot borrow money to pay for your savings. Multiple government programs provide low-interest student loans, and you can always cut student loan interest on your taxes.

Taking out a mortgage on a home. Taking a loan of this amount can be overwhelming, but purchasing a house creates ownership in something that will house you, and generate some retirement money. Even while you struggle to clear your debt, you may consider it an advantage to put any available liquid cash as a deposit, though it may not be the right choice.

A home mortgage interest is cut on your taxes, and the rate of interest is lower on your home loan than on the credit card. In other words, it is important to have money to pay for other expenses instead of credit.

Though purchasing a house was initially considered a strong, future-proof investment, certain homeowners do find themselves on the wrong side on their home mortgage loan. They owe banks more than the value of their homes. However, strategic planning, purchasing only what you can afford, and maintaining low interest by having good credit may allow you to purchase a home that one day you will own completely.

Buying a car. If you don't have public transport in your area, or you cannot manage to get someone with whom you can carpool with, then you may have to consider buying a car. An auto loan can either be "good" or "bad", but the main thing is to ensure that the auto loan is a good debt, so look for the lowest possible rates on your loan. In addition, you need to make a large down payment while ensuring that you remain with some cash on hand just in case you need it.

Your best goal should be to go for a used car model instead of a brand-new one, possibly saving yourself thousands on the sticker price and the interest that is paid throughout the loan.

Business loans. While this may not be seen as good debt, borrowing money to begin a business or expand a business is perhaps a great idea if the business is thriving. After all, you need money to make more money, right?

Sometimes, you may have to borrow capital to employ new people, purchase a new device, pay for advertisement, or even develop the first new widget you designed. The point is that you borrow this money to expand the business or increase income, then this will count as good debt.

What is Bad Debt?

Bad debt is that which depletes your wealth and isn't affordable. Plus, it provides no means to pay for itself.

Bad debts may have no realistic repayment plans and usually deplete when people buy things at an impulse. If you aren't sure whether you can repay the money, then don't borrow the money because that will be a bad debt.

Examples of bad debt

The credit card debt. A typical household in the United States has a balance of more than $10,000 on their credit card every month. However, the debt usually increases faster than we may realize and is always used to purchase things that we want instead of need. It is easier to think that you can afford something using a card than paying it with cash.

Borrowing from a 401K. When you ask for money from a 401K program, you will need to chat with the IRS, and if you aren't using the money to purchase a home, you will need to pay the loan in five years. If you fail to pay it back, you risk being charged with a severe penalty. Also, the interest that you pay on the loan will get taxed twice.

You can't get a loan to fund your retirement. For that reason, borrowing money from your retirement plan to use it to pay for anything that isn't part of retirement is a bad idea. You will be putting your retirement at risk when you get a loan from a 401k, so don't make this mistake.

Payday loans. It may appear easy to borrow money from payday loan firms, but it is hard to pay it back. These companies offer loans with very high interest rates. The companies take advantage of the fact that many people need that money. As a result, borrowing a small amount may end up costing you a lot.

Payday loans aren't considered the worst kind of debt that you can take on. If you really need a short-term loan, it is better to go for a cash advance on a credit card rather than borrow money from these firms.

Using consolidation or settlement strategies to pay down debts

Debt consolidation is another strategy that can be used to manage your debts. It involves combining two or more debts at a lower interest rate than you are currently at.

But it is worth doing your research and making some phone calls to see if there is a company that's willing to work with you. If you can lower your monthly bill to a manageable level, at an interest rate that's reasonable, that can make all the difference in handling your debt.

Like many strategies, you have had the option of settling your debts with companies for decades. Lenders always want as much money as you can give them versus being shafted for the entire amount in a bankruptcy. It is just that consolidation and settlement options rose in popularity during the recent financial crisis making it appear in more articles and news pieces than ever before.

CONCLUSION

You should now have a better idea of how to repair your credit with or without using section 609. While many people feel that this is one of the best ways to get rid of your bad credit, there are a lot of situations where writing a dispute letter will not help you gain better credit. For example, if you have missed payments on your credit cards within a certain amount of time. Even if the credit card company states that you didn't pay during the months you did, this is something that won't work to dispute because you have recently missed payments.

In the times we live in, it is almost impossible to live without having at least one credit. The unstable rates of unemployment can affect everyone, which is why more and more Americans are confronted with the problem of bad credit. What you have to understand is that bad credit gets even worse over time as its grave consequences will be felt more and more, leading to things such as the impossibility to get a new credit, refinance an old credit, rent an apartment or get a job. This is why you should act in a time and take care of your finances, especially in the context of a shaky national and international economy.

When it comes to struggling with credit card debt, the best way to start repairing your credit is to make sure you understand the federal laws associated with credit card debt. Be assured that you have been protected and that the credit card company is not doing anything illegally. If everything is legal, then you simply want to work on paying off your credit card payments.

You will want to come up with a financial plan which will help you start to pay off your debt strategically. You then want to make sure that, no matter what, you follow this plan. Even if you find yourself in an emergency after a few months when your car breaks down, you want to find another way to come up with your emergency funding. It is important that you continue to make more than the minimum payment on time with all your credit cards. The fewer fees you need to add into your balance, the quicker you will be able to pay off your credit card debt.

While many people don't realize this, most credit card companies want to work with you. The number one reason for this is they want to keep you as a customer, basically, so they can continue receiving your money. One strategy to use is to call and say that you would like to close your account. They will then try to focus on keeping your account open, which usually results in them dropping a few missed payments or over the limit fees. Another strategy to use is simply to explain to them what happened, why you were late, and tell them that you want to put your account in good standing. They are usually willing to drop some fees or so much money if you are willing to pay a certain amount off that day.

Remember to be consistent and make sure to rid yourself of all the unnecessary expenses that you have. Try to establish a new and fresh way to keep track of your payments. Do not be afraid to act, for it is only then that you will be able to see the result. Always think positive, and do not let failure hold you back from your goal to be credit worthy once again. In the end, all the efforts are truly worth it. Not only will you have peace of mind and feel better about your life, but the more important goal is to have a trouble-free process in acquiring a new house or car because of your good and trustworthy credit. What is more, because of that good credit standing, you might even land the job or start the business that you have been dreaming of. Isn't that something to look forward to?

If you decide to write a dispute letter under section 609 because you have noticed that information which reflects negatively on your credit score is over seven years old, then you should follow the tips and guidelines. You want to make sure that you do your best when writing this letter. Don't feel that it is just a simple letter and write it quickly. Make sure that you have all the information you need, all the documentation, you proofread the letter, and certify the letter with a receipt request. Keep all the correspondence that you receive and that you send, keep your original copies, and anything else. You want to have a thorough paper trail.

You also have a set budget which you follow every month. This includes ways that you are increasing your emergency fund, so you can think about safely closing your last credit card account and no longer even have credit cards on your mind. With every credit card offer you receive in the mail; you immediately shred and then recycle the paper.

You are living comfortably and growing your savings. You have finally reached financial freedom.

CREDIT SCORE SECRETS

Improve Your Business or Personal
Finance with This Ultimate Guide
to Boost Your Credit Score.
Learn How to Manage Your
Money and Change
Your Mindset in Few Easy Steps.

By: Dave Rich

TABLE OF CONTENTS

CREDIT SCORE SECRET

Credit Score

30% Amounts Owed

10% New Credit

FICO°SCORE

15% Length of Credit History

35% Payment History

10% Credit Mix

Credit simply means your ability to borrow. As such, your credit score is a numerical representation of the risk a lender faces if they were to lend money to you. It is based on the analysis of one's credit files/history. Another layman's definition is that it is the difference between being denied credit and being granted credit. Well, since money is often scarce, borrowing becomes a great option for sourcing funds to do whatever you want to do. It simply enables you to do things you would otherwise not afford if you were to be paying in cash. The credit score determines how lenders perceive you when advancing credit. When your score is high, it means you are a reliable borrower so you won't need to pay more but when the score is low, the lenders treat you with caution and charge you more to advance credit to you. The cost of borrowing (interest you pay) is usually linked to your credit score. In other terms, the credit score determines how much you pay for a mortgage, health insurance, car insurance, and lots of other things including your utilities, cell phones, car payments, etc. Employers also look into credit scores lately before hiring, which means this can determine whether you are hired or not. As you may have noticed, if your score is not good, your life can be pretty much a nightmare. You will probably not even fathom the idea of living in your dream home, or driving your dream car because getting these will be literally out of your reach. Don't get me wrong, these people that run from their debts are not bad people. Maybe they have a reason to stop paying off their debts. While a few missed payments may seem harmless, it actually does your permanent damage.

This damage becomes apparent when you try to borrow money from lenders, or when you get a new credit card. The fact that you missed some payments is permanently reflected on your credit score.

The Purpose of Credit Scores

Credit scores are designed to mitigate various types of risk. The most commonly mentioned risk is that of lending money to a borrower. It determines one's credit worthiness i.e., how lending money to you is risky. Here is a summary of why credit scoring is great.

- Credit scores allow people to get loans faster (almost instantly) since lenders can speed up the approval process. It is possible to make instant credit decisions if you are a lender, which means this helps borrowers to access credit fast.
- It is an objective way of making credit decisions: This focuses on facts rather than feelings which are unverifiable.
- There is more credit: Lenders approve more loans based on credit.
- Lower credit rates: There are more lenders (credit), which increases competition thus pushing the cost of credit lower.

Why should your credit score be high?

Cheaper credit: Lenders are more willing to offer a lower interest rate. Here is a practical scenario:

- A credit score of 750 translates to a 6.11 interest on a 30-year $300,000 mortgage, while a credit score of 620 translates to a 7.42 interest on the same mortgage. As you can see, this difference will definitely translate into thousands of dollars over the 30-year mortgage period.
- It puts you on an equal footing with creditors and lenders. You can comfortably negotiate knowing that lenders are competing to have you as their good risk borrower.
- In addition, businesses develop interest in your business because it is a high value asset courtesy of the low risk.

- Insurance companies also request your credit report before deciding your premiums or even whether they will cover a risk for you.

What is a FICO Score?

The credit score structure was formulated by the Fair Isaac Corporation also referred to as FICO. This credit score is utilized by financial institutions. There is other credit score models; however, the FICO score is the one that is most commonly used. Consumers can get and keep high credit scores by simply making sure their debt level remains low, and they maintain an extended history of paying their bills as and when they are due.

In the FICO scoring formula, not all credit reports are scored equally.

Credit scores are weighted based on the particular "score card" that a person falls under.

For example, if the person has filed for bankruptcy, they may be scored using a special "bankruptcy" scorecard.

The credit score for a person under one scorecard may be affected differently by s negative event, like a late payment, then of someone with the same event on a different scorecard.

The score card you're on is determined by the most recent significant event in your credit history.

The first 10 scorecards go something like this...

Scorecards 1-5:

1. Those with public records, including judgments and bankruptcy, on their credit report
2. For those with serious delinquencies other than bankruptcies (60, 90, 120 latest, collections, judgments, charge-offs repossessions, etc.).
3. Those with only 1 credit account (very thin files)
4. Those with only 2 credit accounts (thin files)
5. Those with 3 credit accounts only.

Scorecards 6-10 should NOT have ANY grave felonies (the definition of "serious" is unknown)

6. 0-2 year's oldest account
7. 2-5 year's oldest account
8. 5-12 year's oldest account
9. 12-19 year's oldest account
10. 19+ years oldest account

There is a total of 12 score cards, and they are subject to change as FICO (formerly Fair Isaac Corp) updates their scoring formula.

How Do You Check Your Credit Score?

It's a common misconception that you will automatically get your credit score when you get a copy of your credit report. This is not entirely the case. Credit reports usually do not include your credit score. It's also important to note that you do not have only one credit score. You will have at least three and more if you include the Vantage Score. They should similar in range but will not usually be the same number because they are an estimate based on a series of calculations.

There are a few different ways you can try to access your credit scores. Look to our list for suggestions:

1. Check with your financial institutions. Many loaners such as credit card companies show your credit score as part of your account for free. If your creditors do not offer this, then you might be able to find the information on your online banking. Wells Fargo, for example, updates your credit score online once a month and shows how the number has changed, and what is most influencing the score.

2. Just like you can order credit reports, you can also order a copy of your score from the three main credit bureaus, and FICO directly. This is a good option if your banking institution does not offer information or you are doing your yearly credit report check.

3. Some people choose to use credit score services, or free credit monitoring services to keep track of their credit score. Others offer greater resources and protection that charge, but there are many free ones. These are good options for those who are looking to keep track of their credit but don't want to spend the extra money for monitoring or to order directly from FICO.

What is a Good Credit Score? How Can I Improve My Credit Rating and Credit Score?

Your credit score is split into several levels, but generally ranges from 300 to 850. The different credit rating levels are label as follows:

- 300 to 600: Bad Credit
- 600 to 649: Poor Credit
- 650 to 699: Fair Credit
- 700 to 749: Good Credit
- 750 + 850: Excellent Credit

The higher your credit score, the better. Better scores allow you to get credit easier, and with lower interest rates. Even when not getting credit, such as when you are renting an apartment, having a better credit rating builds trust with potential landlords.

The best thing that you can do to get your credit score up is to make payments on time. As soon as you start missing payments, your score will plummet. A delinquency can turn into a negative item that is much harder to remove. If you do miss payments, communicating and maintaining a good relationship with your creditor is key.

INCREASING YOUR FICO CREDIT SCORE

When you improve your credit score, you can save thousands of dollars later when you get offered improved rates and terms on loans, credit cards, and mortgages. This process of repairing and improving your credit score is not something that happens overnight.

Ways to Improve Your Score

While some steps don't work overnight, if you are diligent enough to work on all of them, you are bound to see a steady pace of improvement over time. This growth is, however, dependent on your making your payments when they are due and consistently paying off your debts. However, if you are trying to rebuild your credit score, you might run into difficulty when applying for a new credit card. You can do something.

Even if you know how to improve your score, there are times when unforeseen credit disasters can occur and wreck the score you worked so hard to build.

Simple Steps to Fix Your Credit Score

The following are the steps to steadily work towards a debt-free future and improve credit score.

Step 1: Look for Any Errors on Your Credit Report

You might wonder what the difference is between a credit score and a credit report. Well, a credit report is a report that contains every piece of data used to determine what your credit score is. That being said, there can be mistakes when calculating your score. It has been known that about 21% of people have errors on a minimum of one of their reports. This means almost a quarter of people with credit scores are suffering from a lower score due to errors.

Step 2: How to Dispute Errors

Below is a guide on how to dispute errors with the three largest credit bureaus.

When you want to dispute an item, you will have to write to the credit reporting agency, telling them that you want to dispute an item or more than one item found in your credit report. It is crucial that you include the reason you are disputing.

Once done, your request should be sent in a letter through certified mail. It is also essential to request a return receipt. This ensures that the credit agency in question has received your dispute. Make sure you maintain copies of any letters that you send, as well as the items you attach. Doing this obligates the credit reporting agency to investigate and check if your dispute holds water. This typically happens over 30 days.

If a company gave your financial information to the credit bureau, it also has to investigate and submit the results. If the dispute is found to be accurate and warranted, the three credit reporting bureaus must be informed, so the mistake can be resolved. Once all of this is done, the credit reporting bureau sends the results to you. Should the resolved dispute influence your credit score, you are obligated to receive a free copy of that report by the company. This free report is not part of the yearly copy you are entitled to.

Step 3: What Makes Up a FICO Score?

An individual has many credit scores; however, the most prominent of them that is relied on by the majority of lenders is the FICO Score. Being able to comprehend the variables that determine how it is calculated can ensure that you are informed on the actions that either positively or negatively affect your score. When you concentrate on the large things listed below that can positively influence your score, you can make a significant impact for it to rise.

You might wonder, what exactly goes into the number that is available to you on your credit report? This consists of some important variables.

- Well, 35% of that is derived from your history of payments. How quickly your payments were made, if your balance was paid off each time, or if you only made payments that met the minimum are all part of the variables considered. It is ideal to pay your entire balance off; however, if you are unable to, you should know that paying slightly more than the minimum can help chip away at the debt, which in turn helps to raise your credit score.
- 30% of the FICO score is calculated using the amount you owe. When you owe almost your entire available credit limit, or you have a lot of debt spread across numerous credit cards, this can cause your credit score to decrease. You should focus on sorting out your most substantial debt first. Once this is paid off, you should use the same payment amount you used to clear the next debt to sort out the second largest. This process is called the snowball effect. This overtime, this helps you to not only pay your massive debt off, but it can also positively influence your credit score.
- 15% of the FICO score is derived from your credit history and how long it has been active. In theory, it might seem like opening numerous credit cards or moving to cancel those cards once they are paid off might sound like a beautiful idea. The truth, however, is that it isn't. It can negatively

affect your FICO score. The best thing to do is to have only a few cards, and older accounts should be kept open longer. Doing this helps to provide you established credit history. It also aids your loan or credit application process as lenders want to see that you have a responsible credit history. And while the percentage accounted for this part of your FICO score is not as big as the ones derived from your payment history, or the amount you owe, it is much more effective to maintain your oldest credit accounts with almost no balance, as this helps to establish your creditworthiness.

- 10% of the FICO score is derived from new credit. This part of your FICO score checks if you have recently applied for credit such as a credit card, a mortgage, or a car loan. All of this information gets recorded on your credit report.

- 10% of the FICO score is derived if the forms of credits you make use of. There are more ways than just credit cards to develop your score. When you have an array of loans, ranging from mortgages to car loans, you can increase your score.

These are the most pertinent variables that help determine your credit score. It is easy to see that the most significant determinants are the amount of debt you owe and your payment history. This is why it is best to tackle these two first.

Step 4: Activate Auto-pay on Your Cards

It does not matter if you make use of an actual calendar stuck to your wall or if you use your smartphone's app to set an alert, you should do whatever you can to be reminded when payments on your credit cards have to be made. Ensure that you try to pay more than the minimum consistently. When you take into account that the largest determinants of your credit score are your payment history and the size of your debt, it makes sense to pay as much as you possibly can towards your debt.

You should leverage technology to help pay your debts down. The majority of credit card issuers make this process is very simple by letting you activate auto-pay. What this does is connect your credit card to your bank account and a predetermined amount is taken out every month.

You should make extra payments whenever you can. You should not wait for the credit card company to send you a statement. The majority of credit card issuers allow you to make extra payments online should you choose to. This is a recommended way to pay off your balance quicker. Deciding to do this will also require you to not incur additional debt on your credit cards. They should not be used as a crutch, and one thing you should never do is to pay off the debt on one credit card with another. All this does is create a debt cycle than could destroy not only your finances but your credit score, as well. This could also cause you problems when you want to apply for a car loan, mortgage, or a new credit card.

This is not a great future to have, so it makes sense to control your debt, rather than let it build up to the point that you are unable to do much of anything when it comes to applying for credit.

Step 5: Sort out the Largest First

You should work on paying off your most substantial debts first and ensure that when you pay, you pay slightly more than the minimum asked. This is the next step to making your credit score better. It has to do with how you pay off your debt. It is best to tackle the most significant debts first. While it might appear more straightforward to pay off the smaller balances on your credit cards, there are reasons why you shouldn't do that till you pay the largest ones:

You have to understand what precisely a revolving debt is. You also have to understand how it functions. A large part of the FICO credit score is determined by the revolving debt you have. This is the large 30% part of the amount of debt you own. This revolving debt is determined as debt on credit cards that haven't been paid off yet. It is much better to have a smaller figure.

Your balance on your credit card has to be lower than your available credit. The figure that most experts agree on is 30%. For your credit to improve, you should have that figure at no more than 10%. What this means is that, if you have a $1,000 credit limit, you should only have $100 on your card.

Step 6: Do Not Make Late Payments

You should try to avoid missing payments or even contesting them, as this could damage your score. If you have missed payments in a period of 3 to 5 months, your account could be closed by your lender. When this happens, it is referred to as a default. Defaults get recorded in your credit report and it not only lowers your score, but it also makes it more difficult for you to gain credit down the line. The default stays on your record for 6 years. The only way it does not appear is if it was recorded in error.

It gets challenging to miss a payment if you already have auto-pay set up. This helps you avoid things such as penalty interest. However, it is possible to make a mistake or forget. It could be that you have suddenly lost your job and you are unable to pay off your debt. If this is the case, you don't want to stop your payments. The best thing to do would be to call the credit card issuer and briefly explain your situation. You can ask them to take the missed payment marker off your account. This lets you have 30 days counting from the due date before your missed or late payment is reported to the three major credit bureaus.

HOW TO BOOST YOUR CREDIT SCORE

If you are trying to improve your credit score as quickly as possible, ask for a free copy of your credit report and check it as soon as possible. You need to know what is in your credit report before you can find out what you need to do to change it.

Check the credit report

The credit score provides a snapshot of your credit status and is determined by a series of factors that can be divided into the following categories: credit history - How long have you been using credit?

Payment History

Do you have a history of paying on time?

Credit amount - How much do you do and how much do you owe?

Check over your credit report with a fine-tooth comb: verify that the amount due for each account is accurate. And look for all the accounts you paid off that still show as outstanding issues. Pay particular attention to any requests for recent information that you have not authorized. Before an endorsing creditor, or someone pretending to be you, for an account, they will make a request that will be indicated on your credit report.

Checking your credit report on a regular basis, at least once a year, is a good way to collect any cases where you could be the target of identity theft - or the credit bureau has accidentally mixed your story with someone similar name.

Pay early and often (or at least, on time)

Credit reports record payment habits on all types of bills and extended credit, not just credit cards. And sometimes these objects show up on their own official report, but not that of another. Old, unpaid gymnastic odds that only appear on a relationship could be affecting your score without even realizing it.

A full one-third of your score depends on whether you pay your creditors on time. So, make sure you pay all your bills by their due dates, including rent/mortgage, utilities, doctor's bills, etc. Keep documentation (such as checks or canceled receipts) to be able to prove that you have done the punctuality of payments.

The Fair Isaac Corporation, which calculates FICO scores, recommends signing up for payment notices if the lender makes them available. Another approach is to create automatic drafts from your bank account.

Pick up a payment order

When using your cards, try to pay them off as soon as you can (you do not need to wait for the instruction in the mail, but you can pay online at any time). When you have the extra money to pay your balances, focus on the cards that are closest to being maxed out, to benefit your most credit score. Zero in credit card balances that are over 50% of your credit limit. Borrowers who have used up more of their available credit are considered higher risk.

Do not open too many accounts

If you shop at that store, it can often be worth getting your card; otherwise, resist the temptation. What is more, every time you apply for credit the potential lender will check your score. Whenever the credit is selected, other potential lenders worry about the additional debt that they can take on. Sometimes, the act of opening a new account, or even applying for one, can lower the score; have a lot of recent inquiries about your credit report dings your score temporarily. So do not ask for the card often if you want to increase your credit score.

Do not close credit cards

A good idea would be to keep three or four credit card accounts open but use only one or two of them; put away or cut the others. Once you have paid a card, however, keep the account open, even if you do not want to use it anymore. In closing, late accounts or those with a history of late payments can also help, as long as you have paid them in full. Because history is important if you decide to close a couple of accounts, close the most recent ones. The length of your credit history is 15% of your score, so even after paying the sales down, keep the oldest cards open. Be sure to use these cards to make occasional purchases (so pay the bills in full), so the card company does not close the account due to inactivity.

Increase the credit limit

There is a way to increase your credit score that does not involve paying a debt or any of the other more traditional credit score tactics by increasing. Since credit scores are determined, in part, on the difference between the credit limit and the amount of credit used, ask for a higher credit limit. Your chances of increasing it are probably better than you think. Of those applying for a higher credit limit, 8 out of 10 have been approved, according to a recent money survey. While it helps to be over 30, there is a good chance for all adults. To prevent the credit decreased with the request for a higher limit, to ask for the highest credit line increase that does not trigger what is called a difficult request.

By increasing the credit limit, the differential between the amount you are allowed to borrow and the amount you actually make is automatically increased. The larger the spread, the higher the credit score.

The credit utilization report

This spread, known as the credit utilization ratio, is expressed as a percentage. For example, if the limit on the MasterCard is $ 5,000 and you have a budget of $ 4,000, the usage ratio is 80%. If you request a credit line increase and the limit goes up to $ 10,000, suddenly your use is only 40%.

Obviously, the higher the percentage, the worse you look. Experts have long said that using 30% of available credit is a good way to keep your credit score high. More recently, this recommendation has been reduced to 20%. In the $ 5000 MasterCard limit example above, 30% usage would represent a $ 1,500 balance. Increasing the credit limit from $ 5,000 to $ 10,000 would allow a $ 3,000 balance and still maintain 30% utilization. This is also the reason why you should not close your accounts, which will increase the percentage of total available credit that you are using - and which will reduce your score.

Negotiate a lower interest rate

However, the key to this strategy is getting more credit, but no longer using credit. In other words, if the limit goes up to $ 1,000, do not go out and half responsible for it. Think of the push as a way to save money when applying for a car loan, home loan or another form of long-term debt where a high credit score will probably lead to big savings through a rate of lower interest.

THE IMPORTANCE OF A GOOD CREDIT SCORE

We all know how important a good credit score is, but we often don't know how to improve it. A good relationship is significant for enhancing the creditworthiness of the market. It can help you in many ways and talk about your clean background. It reflects your personality and your character. Employers also prefer someone with a good score and a clean relationship. It is synonymous with sensitivity and responsibility. If you're at a loss and don't know how to improve your score, check out our credit guide. This will help you understand the importance of a good score and suggest some ways and means of getting a desirable score.

How to Get Help?

At this point, as you read this article, you may experience the following problems.

- A poor or falling credit rating.
- Think about foreclosure or filing for bankruptcy.
- Invoices or credit card loans over the limit or pending.
- Threats for non-payment of bills, loans or mortgages.

Faced with one of these problems, you can get help from a variety of sources. These financial difficulties are common and can force you to lose your way. Several companies and agents are waiting to attract such gullible customers. They can mislead you and cause you further difficulties. You could work in your interest instead of in your interest. Several agencies of this type have unsatisfied customers who have been deceived. If you want to resolve your situation and work on the current financial situation, you need to read the relevant guide. Here are some ways you can improve your scores.

Tips to Improve Your Score

Plastic Money - The first thing you need to do to improve your score is to stop using plastic money. If you've already created a large invoice, you can order it, but no longer use the card. Reduce your purchases for a while until you are in control of the situation again.

Report - Request a report and rate the area you need to work on. You also need to carefully review the reports to determine if there are errors. Check for incorrect information. Has it corrected by writing to the office about it?

Pay your bills on time - use your salary to pay your bills on time. Don't be late in paying. Late payment not only involves fees and expenses but is also reflected negatively in the relationship. Make sure you pay all your bills on time.

Don't fall victim to scam repair - discover the federal law that governs this system. Some people fall victim to such repair agencies. It is better to face the situation alone. If necessary, contact the State Commission for more information on the procedure. You can also read books on credit. It's important to keep the situation under control before it gets worse and makes you fail.

Importance of a Good Credit Score?

The credit score is a numerical expression for the statistical analysis of credit files. In simple terms, this number will help you prove your creditworthiness. The score measures past ability to repay loans and manage previously granted loans. It is usually based on the reporting information of the credit bureau. You will rely on wounds to reduce losses when it comes to bad debt. It is the outcomes that can determine who is eligible for a loan and which interest rates are most appropriate, including the credit limits that individuals receive.

Credit scores can also say a lot about your character and personality and linger forever. You will never benefit from poor results in financial situations that must occur throughout your life. You can also use numbers to evaluate employers, which makes having a good score very important. It will represent your level of responsibility and sensitivity.

When buying a home: a home is a huge investment that can be very difficult to make. A home loan may be needed to make your dreams come true. With a good loan, you will meet the stringent requirements that banks, like future homeowners, will make it easier for you to get the loan.

When buying a car: vehicle loans are among the most popular. Auto loans don't seem to be home loans. It is, therefore, possible to get along with bad credit scores. However, if you have bad credit, you will end up paying very high yield loans with your auto loan. The deposit is also higher for you if you have a band score.

When starting a business: Just like buying a house or car, financial support may be needed to start a business. The credit rating depends on your eligibility for that loan. This can seriously affect your ability to access a corporate loan when it is needed.

Looking for work: Nowadays, employers also run credit checks when they want to hire new employees. It is especially common in the financial sector and government institutions. A negative score can be an obstacle to this job, so it is important to maintain good credit scores.

You will also find it very important to check your credit report. A thorough review helps to identify errors. You will likewise get numerous tips and guidance on the best way to improve your credit ratings to keep up a cleaner register before you need money or business help. There are excellent websites out there that will help you check and calculate your scores and even get a free copy of them.

Before doing any real estate business, you need to know a few things about your balance. First, a copy of all three credit reports (Trans Union, Equifax and Experian) is required, which can be easily found online in this era of computer information.

The primary concern you need to search for in your momentum reports is the point at which you have recorded antagonistic data. "Unwanted information" includes things like late payments, collections, judgments, etc. If you have negative information about your relationships and have the money to pay for them, do it immediately. The better your credit, the more business you can do. However, as mentioned above, you can do business if you have bad credit. It's easier if you don't.

The accompanying table will enable you to comprehend where your credit is found:

Credit score / rating

700 or more / excellent (A + credit)

This score indicates that in the past three years, there have been no significant delays (60 days or more) for any type of loan payment. These people can get slightly better interest rates on some types of loans.

699-660 / Very good (credit)

659-620 / Voucher (one credit)

These values do not result in significant payments (60 days or more) overdue for a mortgage loan in the past two years and only a few small delays in loan payments over the past two years. These people can quickly get "market interest rates" on all types of loans, including public loans. Bankruptcies must be resolved and resolved for four years to be classified as "good".

619-590 / Fair (credit B)

This score indicates some significant delays (60 or more days) for a mortgage loan in the past two years and widespread minor delays in loan payments over the past three years. These people receive slightly higher interest rates for all types of loans, except for public loans (FHA, VA), which are not based solely on credit scores.

589-480 / Bad (credit C)

This score indicates MANY significant delays (60 days or more) overdue for a mortgage in the past two years and widespread MAJOR payments (60-90 days) for loan payments over the past three years. People with a C loan generally receive higher interest rates and higher equity or a higher down payment for all types of loans except public loans.

In most cases, 520 is the type of approval limit for portfolio loan buyers whose loans are led by actions. Bankruptcies must be paid at the time of applying for a loan to be classified as "bad". Current amortizations, bad debts and sentences sometimes don't have to be repaid to get a mortgage. However, the penalty is a small pool of lenders, high-interest rates and stiff prepayment penalties if you refinance within three years.

Another factor in deciding your financial assessment is the number of solicitations you have. Numerous applications are dismissed because the candidate has an excessive amount of solicitations. As a general rule, "too many" requests are defined as more than 6-8 requests in your credit report. Credit bureaus have informed creditors that a person with more than this in their credit report is jumping around looking for credit, generally indicating that they are desperate or inattentive. Of course, they never think that you could simply look for the best loan.

If you have more than 6-8 requests in your credit reports, the new FCRA (Fair Credit Reporting Act) states that no requests can remain in your report for more than a year. If your report shows previous requests, you can remove duplicate requests.

It is essential to know your balance. If your score is between 620 and 700 or more, you can negotiate better conditions and interest rates on your loans. But if your credit is lower, you can still get credit, but all you have to do is "turn" and take a higher interest rate until your credit improves.

Before doing business, we cannot stress the importance of knowing your balance.

1. A borrower with a score of 680+ is considered for an A + loan. This type of loan includes the essential subscription, probably through a "computerized automated subscription" system, which is completed in a few minutes and can be completed in a few days.

2. A borrower with a score below 680 but over 620 will find that lenders take a closer look when applying for a loan. Additional credit documents and explanations may be requested before making a subscription decision. This evaluation area may allow borrowers to obtain an A loan, but it can take anywhere from a few days to several weeks to complete.

3. A borrower with a score below 620 can be excluded from the best loan rates and conditions. These borrowers are usually redirected to alternative funding sources.

Remember, just because your credit isn't A +, with patience and some creative funding, you can still do the business you want to do. Your credit can and will consistently change, and as you begin working together and reimbursing these loan specialists, it will bit by bit increment. This makes financing your offers simpler and more straightforward. Be quiet and constant and recall the significance of knowing your equalization.

HOW CREDIT SCORES ARE CALCULATED

Your FICO score is a measure of the overall quality of your credit. While it is not the only available metric for determining credit score, it is the one that is most commonly used by a wide range of different lenders and companies when it comes to determining the level of risk that is associated with a given individual.

However, some of the details regarding it have been found out, including the fact that a FICO score is based on a handful of different categories at various levels of importance to the total. It has been determined that payment history is weighted with approximately 35 percent relevance, the amount owed has a 30 percent relevance, credit history length has a 15 percent relevance, abundance of new credit has a 10 percent relevance and the type of credit used has a 10 percent relevance.

Payment history relates to how prompt you have been when it comes to previous payments you have made to various creditors. It also factors in things such as delinquency, number of accounts you have in collections, bankruptcy and how long it has been since these problems appeared on your record. As such, the greater number of problems you have had in this regard, the worse your overall FICO score is going to be.

When it comes to the amount you currently owe to lenders, FICO takes into account the amount of debt you currently have as well as the types of accounts you hold and the number of different accounts that you currently hold.

How is your credit score calculated?

Your FICO score is a measure of the overall quality of your credit. While it is not the only available metric for determining credit score, it is the one that is most commonly used by a wide range of different lenders and companies when it comes to determining the level of risk that is associated with a given individual.

It is based on a handful of different categories at various levels of importance to the total. It has been determined that payment history is weighted with approximately 35 percent relevance, the amount owed has a 30 percent relevance, credit history length has a 15 percent relevance, abundance of new credit has a 10 percent relevance and the type of credit used has a 10 percent relevance.

It also factors in things such as delinquency, number of accounts you have in collections, bankruptcy and how long it has been since these problems appeared on your record. As such, the greater number of problems you have had in this regard, the worse your overall FICO score is going to be.

When it comes to the amount you currently owe to lenders, FICO takes into account the amount of debt you currently have as well as the types of accounts you hold and the number of different accounts that you currently hold.

To help you understand the scores better, here is a breakdown of the credit score ranges and what each means.

720 and Above Excellent

When you have this score, you get the best interest rates and repayment terms for all loans. This score can come in handy if you are hoping to make some major purchases. You will be able to get credit without any problems and at the lowest possible rates. But then, this score is extremely hard to establish. You will have to put in a lot of effort to maintain this score and still, you will not come anywhere close to 800. The most you can wish to come close to is 720 and remain there for as long as possible.

680-719-Good

When you are in this category, you will get good rates and terms but not as good as those with excellent scores. With this score, you can get favorable mortgage terms. You might not face as many problems but will have to be ready to run around from company to company to have your credit approved. Again, this score is not very common. You need to put in extra effort to get it over the 680 mark. If because of some erroneous charges you are not able to cross this limit, then you must try your best to get it cleared as soon as possible.

620-679-Average

When you are in this category, you can get fair mortgage terms and have it easy when buying smaller ticket items, (of course with no better rate than good and excellent scores). Take care not to slip down to the level where mortgage is unaffordable.

580-619-Poor

When you are at this level, you only get credit on the lenders' terms. You will probably pay more to access credit so be ready to pay more. Also, you should remember that you cannot access auto financing if your score goes lower than this range so you should work towards building it. This is where a large majority lie. Their score will be bad mostly owing to wrong entries. If you lie here, then you will have a tough time getting credit in your budget limits and will have to be ready to pay up a lot of money.

500-579-Bad

If your credit score is in this range, access to credit will cost you dearly. Actually, if you are looking for a 30-year mortgage, you could be looking at, at least 3% higher interest rates than how much you would pay if you had good credit. On the other hand, if you are looking for something short time like a 36-month auto loan, you will probably pay almost double the interest rate you would pay if you had good credit. So being here is probably the worst thing that can happen to your credit report. You cannot possibly be here and hope to get away with low interest rates.

Less than 500

If your credit score goes to this level, it is so bad that it might be almost impossible to get any type of financing. If you do, the interest rate will simply be unfathomable. You might have to spend 30 to 40 years trying to repay it. Your entire life will be dedicated toward repaying a loan and you might only get free by the time you are 50.

I am sure several of you are in this last range. But do not panic as help is at hand. You might wonder if it is possible for you to fix your score if you are in this category and the answer is yes! It is possible for you to improve your credit score and possibly enter the good range.

FACTORS THAT AFFECT YOUR CREDIT SCORE

The three main credit bureaus calculate your FICO score when assigning you a credit score. FICO scores are made up of the five key factors of "payment history, current level of indebtedness, types of credit used, length of credit history, and new credit accounts" (Hayes, 2019, para. 1) to calculate your score. Since the biggest companies focus on these factors, bringing up your credit score most commonly involves addressing these areas and making changes where necessary to score better in each field. While all five factors contribute to your overall score, your payment history and your current level of debt are weighted the heaviest, so let's look at these first.

Past Payment History

Your payment history is usually the most important factor in determining your credit score. It supplies information about all of your previous debt payments, including how quickly you paid them off, whether you met all payment due dates on time, if you incurred any late fees, and if you repeatedly missed payments and ended up in collections. This score is calculated using all forms of repayment, which is everything from home mortgages to credit cards to student loan debt. It does not include loans given to you by friends and family, as these loans are not reported to credit bureaus, and typically the only thing you risk by not paying them back in a timely manner is incurring your friends' wrath.

Though it is called a payment history, this does not mean that a few missteps will permanently keep you from a higher credit score. Debts that go to collections and declaring bankruptcies can impact your credit score severely when they occur, but if you proceed to build up many on-time payments and demonstrate that you have changed the way you handle your finances, it can help to balance these less positive events out and even outweigh them.

Payment history gives lenders the best picture of what you are like as a debtor and how much of a risk you would be should they approve you. This is why it accounts for such a large portion of your credit score; in fact, payment history makes up 35 percent of a FICO credit score, which is much higher than any other single factor. The best way to ensure you have a healthy credit score is to make sure your payment history is in order, which you can achieve by always making at least the minimum payments on time and trying not to use the maximum amount of credit granted to you.

Total Amount of Debt

Your level of debt makes up 30 percent of a FICO credit score, making it nearly as influential as your payment history. Having too many outstanding debts can make creditors unwilling to give you a new one, as they are uncertain whether or not you can handle so much debt at a time. For example, if you already owe $80,000 in student loans, it can be hard to get approved for a mortgage on a $300,000 house, as it would saddle you with a very high amount of debt altogether. The higher your total debt, the less likely you are to be able to pay it off, which can make lenders uncertain.

Your debt burden is also impacted by your credit utilization, or the ratio of how much credit you are currently using versus how much is allowed to you. If you have a credit card with a credit limit of $4,000 and you are only using $300, this is going to reflect better than if you were using $3,000 of credit. Credit balances that are maxed out or over the available limit really hurt your score in this category.

Keep in mind that your current income level is not part of your credit score, so even if you make much more than your current debts, they can still harm your score. Say you make $150,000 a year, but you have $30,000 in unpaid credit card debt. You could probably afford to pay a great deal of it, but if you merely make the minimum payment each month, the remainder still counts as outstanding debt. If you can make payments and reduce your debts, you should do so whenever possible.

Length of Credit History

The length of your credit history is based on both the age of each line of credit on your report and how long you have been working on your credit. It makes up 15 percent of your FICO credit score, so it is relatively important, but not a game changer. This is good, because for those who have only just started to build their credit, there is not much you can do to alter this score other than simply wait it out. Younger people often have trouble with this aspect, as many do not consider credit to be a necessity until they encounter a credit roadblock that gets in the way of a purchase. This is why it is always a good idea to start looking at your credit as early as possible.

Having a longer credit history provides a pattern of behavior that showcases a more complete picture of your financial habits. Someone who has only had credit for a few months may be great at paying off their debts on time, but have more difficulty doing so as time goes on. On the other hand, a brief period of financial turmoil is more easily remedied in a longer credit history of making payments on time. This is true for both individual credit lines and your credit history as a whole.

Types of Credit

Different types of credit affect your credit score in different ways, and having a variety of credit sources rather than many of the same kind of lines of credit can help your score. Credit is broken down into three main types known as revolving credit, installment credit, and open credit. Each of these types deals with different sources of loans. Your mix of these different credit types accounts for 10 percent of your FICO credit score. While it is far from the most important factor, having a good balance of credit types can still bring your score up a few points. To do so, you must know what each category of credit means.

The first type, **revolving credit**, is commonly associated with credit cards and home equity loans. It does not require you to make a fixed number of payments, but you are required to pay a minimum balance based on how much debt you have every term, usually monthly. Revolving credit also typically charges interest on unpaid debt, and usually sets a credit limit on how much you can borrow at a time. Aside from your credit limit and monthly payments, revolving credit is relatively unstructured, and allows you to pay off your debts at your own leisure provided you continue to make at least the minimum payment.

Installment credit usually deals with larger loans that you take out for big life events. These can be student loans, auto loans, mortgages, personal loans, or many other kinds. Repayment is much more structured than with revolving credit. Payments are regularly scheduled and require a fixed amount that does not fluctuate under normal circumstances, though certain factors like changes to the terms of your loan or attempts to refinance can alter the amount you are required to pay each period. Most forms of installment credit will take a while to pay off in full, unlike revolving credit, which tends to be much more manageable to pay all at once.

Open credit is much less common than either of the above types, but can still occur, usually in the case of charge cards. The main difference between charge cards and their revolving credit counterparts, credit cards, are how much of the balance needs to be paid off each term. Generally, charge cards and any other forms of open credit require you to pay the entire balance at the end of a payment period, while credit cards usually have a minimum payment that does not account for the entire bill. Open credit typically does not have a spending limit either.

Ideally, you should have at least two different kinds of credit rather than having all your credit be the same type. However, it is not worth opening new accounts just to achieve this goal, as your credit diversity accounts for a low portion of your score and opening too many accounts can negatively impact your credit, negating any positive effects.

Amount of New Credit

This is a less well-known factor, but the number of new credit lines you open within the last year can impact your score. New credit makes up 10 percent of your FICO score, which is not a large percentage but still worth keeping in mind. Oftentimes, especially for younger people and those newer to credit, you will be tempted to open multiple different accounts to start building your credit, but opening too many in a short period can actually harm it. You should try to keep your number of new accounts to just one or two per year if you can, as this will minimize the impact on your score.

Opening new lines of credit can hurt your score because each new line of credit you apply for must check your credit score. Checking your score too frequently can negatively impact it, so too many creditors making credit inquiries can be more trouble than it is worth. Additionally, a new line of credit lowers your length of credit history, a score factor, so you will want to avoid making an unreasonable number of new accounts in a year.

FIXING YOUR CREDIT SCORE FAST

C redit bureaus have 30 days to examine complaints and frequently concede to what lenders state about you, regardless of whether it's valid. Regardless of whether all parties concur that a mistake has been made, the errors can continue to manifest in your file on account of the automated idea of most credit reporting. You may need to contact creditors and the bureaus a few times to get mistakes erased. The process may take weeks; best case scenario, you may be taking on the conflict for quite a long time or even years. In case you're amidst attempting to get a mortgage, these errors can cause significant problems. You probably won't have sufficient opportunity to fix your report before the house drops out of escrow or you stall out with an interest rate a lot higher than you have the right to pay.

Issues, for example, these might entice you to turn to one of the numerous organizations that guarantee "moment credit fix" or that assurance to help your credit score. No authentic organization makes such guarantees or certifications, however, so any individual who employs one of these outfits is asking to be misled. There are, in any case, a developing number of certified administrations that can actually fix your credit report errors in 72 hours or less. Read on to learn more.

Fixing Your Credit in a Matter of Hours: Rapid Rescoring

Rapid rescoring administrations came about in light of the fact that such a large number of people were losing loans or paying an excess of interest on account of credit bureau mistakes. Before you get energized, however, you ought to learn what these administrations can and can't do:

- They can't manage you straightforwardly as a consumer— Rapid rescoring is typically offered by little credit-reporting agencies, which fill in as a kind of go between the bureaus and the lending experts. These agencies, which are frequently free, however, which may be auxiliaries of credit bureaus, provide uncommon administrations for loan officials and mortgage representatives, for example, blended or "3-in-1" credit reports. To profit by rapid rescoring, you should work with a loan official or mortgage representative who buys in to an agency that offers the administration.

- They can help you just in the event that you have proof, or if proof can be obtained—Rapid rescoring administrations aren't intended to help people who presently can't seem to begin the credit-fix process. You need something in writing, for example, a letter from the creditor recognizing that your account was reported as late when you were actually reality on time. (This is one reason that it's so necessary to get everything in writing when you're attempting to fix your credit.) If you don't have such proof, however, the creditor has recognized the error, some rapid recorders can get the proof for you. Nonetheless, that may add days or weeks to the process.

- They can assist you with getting errors fixed; however, they can't remove genuine negative things that are in dispute—also, you need proof that a mistake was made—not simply your say as much. If that the credit bureau is already researching your complaint regarding the error, the item typically cannot be included in a rapid rescoring process.
- They can't vow to support your score—"How Credit Scoring Works," sometimes removing negative items can really hurt a score—strange as that may appear.

The scoring formula attempts to contrast you with people who have comparable credit histories. In the event that you've been lumped into the gathering with a bankruptcy or other dark spots on your report, you may find that your score falls when a portion of those negative items are removed. Rather than being at the highest point of the bankrupts' gathering, as such, you've dropped to the base of the following gathering—the people who have better credit. All the more commonly, removing an error probably won't help your score as much as you may have trusted and probably won't win you a superior interest rate. There are no assurances with rapid rescoring.

Quite a long time ago, brokers and other lending professionals could take care of these problems. In the days prior to the widespread utilization of a credit score, a broker or loan officer could mediate to persuade a lender to disregard mistakes or little imperfections on a client's credit file. Everybody included comprehended that credit report errors were common, and having an accomplished loan pro vouch for your creditworthiness could frequently complete an arrangement.

With the coming of credit scoring and automated loan processes, however, those chances to advocate for clients quickly evaporated. Lending professionals shared consumers' dissatisfaction when incorrect information continued to be reported by the bureaus—information that frequently hosed credit scores and brought about more awful rates and terms than the borrower merited. The mortgage brokers needed an approach to slice through the bureaucracy and accelerate the process. Free credit reporting agencies, with their littler, specific staffs, started to fill the need. Here's the means by which it works. Your broker loan or officer obtains evidence from you that a mistake has been done, and he sends that proof to the credit agency that provides the rapid rescoring service.

The recorders, thusly, have uncommon associations with the credit bureaus that enable their requests to be handled quickly. The rescoring service transfers proof of errors to unique departments at the credit bureaus, and the departments contact the creditors (typically electronically). In the event that the creditor concurs that an error was made, the bureaus quickly update your credit report. After that occurs, another credit score can be calculated. The expense for this service is typically somewhere close to $50 and $100 for each "trade line" or account that is remedied, albeit a few agencies provide the rescoring for no additional charge, as part of a part of services provided to lending professionals.

The presence of rapid rescoring does not change the way that you should be proactive about your credit. Months before applying for any loan, you have to order copies of your reports and start testing any errors. You likewise need to keep your correspondence about these errors. All things considered; rapid recorders typically require some kind of paper trail to pursue to prove to the bureau that the mistakes in fact exist. In any case, if that you wind up highly involved with getting a mortgage and an old problem repeats, rapid rescoring can assist you with disposing of the problem and spare the arrangement.

All in all, how would you discover one of these services? In case you're already managing a loan officer or mortgage broker, ask whether she approaches a rapid rescoring service. If that your lending pro has never known about rapid rescoring—it's an ongoing enough advancement that some haven't—request that her contact the agency that provides her organization with credit reports to check whether it's accessible.

Boosting Your Score in 30 to 60 Days

Rebuilding your credit can sometimes be an excruciatingly slow process, yet you can take a couple of easy routes that may increase your score in as meager as a month or two, as talked about in the accompanying segments.

Pay Off Your Lines of Credit & Credit Cards.

Probably the fastest approaches to support a score is to lower your debt use proportion—the distinction between the amounts of revolving credit that is accessible to you and the amount that you're utilizing. One straightforward approach to improve your proportion is to redistribute your debt. In the event that you have a big balance on one card, for instance, you could transfer probably a portion of the debt to different cards. It's usually better for your scores to have little balances on a number of cards than a big balance on a solitary card. You additionally could explore getting a personal installment loan with your nearby credit association or bank, and utilize the cash to pay down your cards. Applying for the loan may affect your scores a piece; however, that is probably going to be more than offset by the development to your scores from lessening the balances on your credit cards. (Credit scoring formulas are substantially more delicate to the balances on revolving debt, for example, credit cards, than to the balances on installment loans.)

Utilize Your Credit Cards Lightly

A big difference between your balances and your limits is what the scoring formula likes to see —and it doesn't really care whether you pay off your balances in full each month or carry them from month to month. What makes a difference is the amount of your credit limits you're really utilizing at some random time. A few people demand they've supported their scores by paying off their cards in full a couple of days before their announcement closes. In the event that their credit card backers, as a rule, send out bills around the 25th, for instance, these people check their balances online about seven days prior and pay off whatever's owed, in addition to a couple of bucks to cover any charges that may manifest before the 25th. When the bills are really printed, their balances are pretty close to zero. (In

163

the event that you utilize this method, simply make sure you make a second payment after your announcement shows up if your balance isn't already zero. That will make sure you don't get damaged with late charges—and truly, that can occur, despite the fact that you made a payment before in the month.)

Concentrate on Correcting the Big Mistakes on Your Credit Reports

If that another person's bankruptcy, collections, or charge-offs are showing up on your report, you will probably profit by having those removed. If that an account you closed is reported as open, then again, you'll probably need to disregard it. Having an account filed as "closed" on your file can't support your score and may hurt it.

Utilize the Bureaus' Online Dispute Process

Some credit-fix veterans swear they get faster results along these lines, however regardless, you'll have to make printouts of all that you send to the bureaus and each correspondence you get from them.

Check whether You Can Have Your Creditors Update Positive Accounts or to Report

Not all creditors report to every one of the three bureaus, and some don't report reliably. If that you can get a creditor to report an account that is in good standing; however, you may see a quick knock in your score.

INCREASE CREDIT LIMIT

One of the least utilized strategies for lowering your debt utilization is a credit limit increase.

All you need to do is call your lender and ask if a credit limit increase is available for your account. Most people don't know that a customer service representative will pull up your entire account before they even answer the phone. They use caller ID to identify you, then have you prove your identity. Once proven, they have all your past conversations, your limits, balances, and possible upgrades available.

They just won't tell you unless you ask. By requesting a credit limit increase you're effectively increasing your available credit without increasing your balance.

For example, if you have one card with a $500 limit and $250 balance, then you're at 50% utilization.

If you get a $500 limit increase, then you have $1000 limit with a $250 balance. That brings your utilization down to only 25% instantly!

The lower your utilization, the higher your scores. With a secured card you simply increase your deposit.

For a regular credit card, make sure you make timely payments for at least 6 months, though 9 months is better. Make sure you keep your card under 50% utilization on all your cards. They won't approve you if you're maxed out or have missed payments within the past year. If they ask you what you're going to use the money for, don't say gambling, or anything irresponsible.

Say you're trying to improve your FICO scores or that you just got a raise and wanted to buy some new furniture. If they ask how large an increase you would like, ask them how much you qualify for. They can tell you after a minute or so.

If you're approved, then you just raised your credit scores with a phone call.

Become an Authorized User

A very simple yet effective technique for boosting your credit scores it to "piggyback" on someone else's credit history and become an Authorized User (AU) on their account.

An AU account is not like a Joint Account.

With a Joint Account both you and the primary holder can add to the credit balance, but you're also both liable for the debts.

If, for example, the primary files for bankruptcy protection, then you will be on the hook for the full balance.

You should avoid Joint accounts at all costs.

With an Authorized User account, only the primary card holder is liable for the debt.

However, the trade line appears on BOTH credit reports.

This is a great way to start your children's credit education, too.

The overnight addition to a credit's age, limit, and payment history can boost a score hundreds of points.

AU accounts are so effective for boosting credit scores that many unscrupulous credit services actually sell them as "Seasoned Trade lines".

First of all, buying a trade line for the purpose of qualifying for financing, like a home mortgage, is fraud. You could go to jail or receive a hefty fine.

Second, FICO knows about Seasoned Trade lines and has made adjustments. When those adjustments hit the scoring model lenders use, then those trade lines will become worthless.

Third, you don't need to buy trade lines anyway. Simply ask a family member, or someone you've shared an address with, to add you as an AU.

Tell them you don't need or want a card, but you want your credit score to benefit from their good credit history.

Look for a card from a major lender with a high limit, low balance, and perfect payment history. The older the card the better.

Refinance Revolving Debt

Any time you pay off your credit cards your score is going to go up.

Refinancing your revolving debt with an installment loan is a way to game the system into thinking you have less debt.

FICO doesn't give as much weight to installment loans, so adding the equivalent installment debt while paying off revolving debt will have an overall positive effect on your score.

Just don't go running up your cards while you're paying off your installment loan or you'll end up with twice the debt.

That's a recipe for disaster.

Day 16 - Refinance Revolving Debt with a Home Equity Loan

Using a Home Equity Loan (HEL) to pay off your revolving debts will improve your credit scores for the same reason using any other installment loan to pay off your revolving debt would work.

FICO gives less weight to installment loan debt.

You just need to make sure you use a Home Equity LOAN and not a Home Equity Line of Credit (HELOC).

A HELOC is scored just like a credit card by FICO, so using it wouldn't improve your scores.

Just be sure to use it to pay down your debt and not as a way to get yourself into more debt.

If you're not disciplined enough to not run up your balances again, then this would not be a smart move for you.

I include it because it works, but you have to pick and choose what works for YOU.

Credit Builder Loans

Some lenders offer a secured loan program designed to help you rebuild your credit.

They're called Credit Builder Loans.

This is a very effective, all be it slow, method for boosting your scores. It's slower because it's an installment loan. Installment loans have less of an impact on your credit score.

Be that as it may, over 6-12 months you will see a credit score increase. That's because you need a few installment loans to improve the "Credit Mix" which is responsible for 10% of your credit score.

Here's how your scores are determined:

FICO SCORES IMAGE

Ideal ratio is:

2-4 credit cards

A car loan, home loan, and personal loan

1-2 retail cards

The credit builder loan completes the personal loan portion of the equation.

Here's how it works;

The amount you borrow is deposited into an escrow account. You can't touch it until the loan is paid. You make your regular payments each month, building your credit score as you go. When you're done paying, you get the full balance plus interest, to do with as you please.

Traditional features include:

Loan amounts from $500-$3000

12-24-month terms

Loan funds earn dividends

Loan interest rate is fixed at 5%

So, for example, a $1000 loan at 5% over 18 months would equal payments of $57.79.

The terms may change from bank to bank so you need to shop around.

WHAT DETERMINES YOUR CREDIT SCORE?

We understand there are credit companies, credit, credit bureaus, and so on. But who does the calculation, what if it is wrong, how do they even determine your actual credit score?

What Determines Your Credit Score?

First, a credit score is a 3-digit figure that summarizes your chances of paying up a loan. It is a score generated based on particular statistics on your credit record, and you would usually get your credit score on your credit report.

Your credit score is not static. It changes according to the situation for which you have requested a credit report. As a practical example, you may request your credit report when getting into a dealership contract a get a 679 score. Then, you find 790 when you request your credit report towards a mortgage. You might say, it is situation-specific. But that is not all. It is also determined by the scoring model adopted in calculating your credit score. What does that even mean? I am about to tell you, trust me.

As FICO had proven your credit report contains four vital bits of information. Since these factors are all that make up your credit report, whatever gives your score must be something among them. Logical, right? Great. So, let's examine these factors according to their sections:

Personally, Identifiable Information (PII)

Your personal information is the first segment you will hit on your credit profile. According to FICO, your PII would include your full name, social security number, and date of birth. That is not all; your gender, location, business, and employer information are also included. You will also find a personal statement section. So that you know; your personally identifiable information is merely for the records. It is to guarantee that the credit transactions are yours, and they are not jumbled up even when there is someone who bears your exact name. You don't get a single score from this. Onto the next!

Credit History.

Okay. Here is the next phase. The credit account section is where you find the most essential details about all of your credit transactions. The details of all your credit accounts are documented here. For example, if you've got at a credit card loan with a credit union. Necessary to add, you will find details of your auto loan, mortgage, business loans, and so on in this section. But this is only IF your loan is still active and documented.

As I have shown earlier. There are chances that you could get a loan that would never reflect on your credit. It is also possible that you get a loan, and round off the payment before calling for your credit report. In that case, the loan will be reflected on your credit report. A concise breakdown of how you paid that loan will also be reflected. This means the credit report will be meticulous enough to tell any reader whether you have promptly paid the previous loan in line with the terms you agreed with the credit union OR not. That may not be good news, so you have got to take the rule of every loan earnestly.

Another thing, all of your credit transactions can't reflect on your credit report. The first type of such are off-the-table transactions that I have told you about; your transaction with friends, unregistered companies, and private credit transactions in general. You need to know that credit companies often require a credit report. They are always interested in other loans you have taken at some point. So, if you have taken no loan earlier and you are looking forward to one, it makes perfect sense to start with a credit card. Draw credits even when you don't need them, but make them minimal and clear them as soon as you can. It gives banks a sense of warmth and assurance. You paid back early because you hate owing. You also drew a loan because you are not an alien to loans, even when you don't need so much of it.

That is out. The next set of loans that may not reflect on your credit report are withdrawn debts. Withdrawn debts are debts that have been found irrelevant, wrong, and in some way, unworthy to be fitted to your records. So, it gets skimmed out. For example, you have just received a claim that you took some credit from Sam Credit Union. If you refute it and the company can't prove that you have some existing loans with them, that record gets scrapped. Even in cases when you took that loan in reality, and you are sure that your creditor or credit union does not have ample information to back that loan, that record will be shucked off when you call for that.

In previous cases, many businessmen took a loan from their friends and made it reflect on their credit report. Their friends may tick that loan as paid, so it gives a positive impression in the credit records, even when it is just make-believe. They find some way to settle the debts of the records. That sounds like a trick to boost a positive impression on your profile. But it's not always so. According to a business magazine, many of such cases got to court because the businessman refused to pay that debt, assuming his friend has got no proofs. Again, these friends may get into a dispute over some other issues and decide to expose each other. Even couples went down in the dumps and exposed each other. So, this may not be a great idea.

Drawing this to a close, I should tell you that bad credit and public records can also be removed from your records. If you have declared bankruptcy, had horrible court decisions on your credit, and so on, they are removed from your credit report after some time. Once this time lapses, you can hold out for their removal and wipe them off your credit records permanently.

Credit Inquiries

Next is Credit Inquiries. As Latoya Irby, a credit analyst, chooses to put it; Credit Inquiries is a general term that covers all investigations and requests for your credit report. As you now understand, credit companies want you to have a credit report before accessing their services; as such, you are bound to create a credit report before you get real loans. But the credit companies don't just want you to set the records. They want to explore it.

For example, if A/B Company had requested your report at some point, and KYC Company had also requested, JJC Company will find these companies in your credit report when you apply for another credit with them. That way, they can tell the other people you have contacted, how 'desperate' you have been finding some credit, and how unsuccessful you have been. That may not be an impressive spotlight.

Public Records

As a practical example, if you have had a dispute and court cases on a credit transaction, it will be shown here. In the case that you have declared bankruptcy, foreclosure, et cetera, these situations will also be displayed at this section of your credit report.

Depending on what you have got here, this may be a plus or a curse to your loan application. But it doesn't matter so much. This is one of the records that can be evicted from your records at some point. Some records take seven years; some take ten before you can get them off. Yet, they will be off at some point. So, if you got some depressing ones already, keep your cheeks alive.

Now, we have extensively worked over the elements in your credit report. We can talk about which of them determines your credit score. Shall we? Great!

As we have earlier identified, credit scores are determined by Credit Scoring Models. What are those?

Credit Scoring Models

These are specialized agencies that develop scoring formats for credit bureaus. According to the Federal Statistics, there are over 50 of them in the United States. Of that, only FICO, a model designed by Fair Isaac Company, is widely used and accepted everywhere. It is often adopted by the three most popular credit bureaus in the country too. Fairly, FICO is trailed by Vantage, Community Empower, Transunion, Xpert, Insurance, and some others.

Due to this diversity, it is impossible to generate an all-purpose method of calculating credit scores. So, it would be impossible to tell how each company measures your credit performance concisely. It is clear however, these scoring models usually generate 3-digit as your credit score, which means you may rank anywhere between 300- 850 (or 950).

ALL ABOUT YOUR CREDIT SCORE

Your credit report is actually more complicated than it may appear at first glance, simply because you are actually dealing with reports from three different agencies, Transunion, Experian and Equifax. What this means is that you will need to check each of the three reports on a regular basis to ensure you have all the pertinent information on your current credit score.

Anatomy of a credit report

While the three major credit reports are going to vary somewhat, information is always going to be grouped into four major categories, these are credit inquires, creditor information, public record information and personal information.

Personal information: The is going to include things like you name and any aliases you use, your social security number, date of birth, employment information and your current and previous addresses.

Public record information: This will include any currently pending legal issues related to your current financial situation. This can include bankruptcies, wage garnishments, judgments and liens. A Transunion report will also show the approximate date when these details will be removed from your report.

Creditor information: This will show all of your debts that have been turned over to a collection agency and all of the lines of credit that you currently have. Additionally, you will find details outlining the status of the account in question, if you share responsibility on any of the accounts, your current balance, payment history, credit limit and if the account is currently past due. Typically, positive and negative accounts will be grouped together.

If you have accounts that are negatively affecting your credit, it is important to keep in mind that you can dispute any of these issues with the credit reporting company. Barring that they will fall off your report after the issue has been resolved for seven years.

Each of your accounts can be classified in the following ways: if any of your accounts are listed as charged off, that means that the account has been written off from the creditor as a loss. While this means you may not have to pay off the account, it will still show up on your credit report for seven years. A revolving account is the classification given to credit cards, you don't need to pay these in full each month and can instead revolve them and just pay the interest.

An installment account is the classification given to loans or other accounts that involved fixed payments. An open account is the classification given to accounts that force you to pay the total balance off each month. A collection account is the classification given to any account that has been transferred to a debt collection agency, this will even show on accounts that you have settled the debt for in the past seven years.

Credit inquiries: This part of your credit report includes a list of every agency that has reviewed your credit report in the past seven years. There are two different types of inquiries, hard inquiries and Soft inquiries.

Credit report codes: The following is a list of codes you may see on your credit report and what they mean.

- CURR ACCT: This means the account is in good standing and current.
- CUR WAS 30-2: This means the account is currently in good standing but has been late by 30 days or more at least twice.
- PAID: This means the account is currently inactive and has been paid off
- CHARGOFF: This means the account has been charged off.
- COLLECT: This means the account has been sent to collections.
- BKLIQREQ: This means the debt has been forgiven due to bankruptcy.
- DELINQ 60: This means the account is at least 60 days past due.

The Fair Credit Acts

When you are going about trying to fix your credit, it can often feel as though the deck is stacked against you, however, the truth of the matter is that there are several laws that can help you to even the odds when it comes to dealing with both creditors and credit bureaus.

FCRA: The FCRA does more than just provide you with a free credit report each year, it also regulates the various credit reporting organizations and helps to ensure that the information they gather on you is both accurate and fair. This means that if you see inaccurate information on your credit report, and report it to the relevant agency, they are legally required to look into the matter and resolve it, typically within 30 days. The same applies to agencies or organizations that generally add details to your credit report. Finally, if an organization that reviews your credit report decides to charge your more or declines to do business with you based on what they find in your report, they are legally obligated to let you know why and what report they found the negative information in.

While this won't help you with that particular lender, if the information is inaccurate you will at least know where to go to clear up the issue. Additionally, if you report an inaccuracy and the credit reporting agency ignores your request you can sue them to recover the damages or a minimum of $2,500. You may also be able to win an additional amount based on punitive damages and legal fees and any other associated costs. You must file legal proceedings within 5 years of when this occurs.

Fair Credit Billing Act: This federal law is part of what is known as the Truth in Lending Act. Its purpose is to provide safeguards to consumers when it comes to unfair billing and make it clear how any errors must be corrected. This law is useful if you are charged for things you didn't purchase, are charged an inaccurate amount for products or services, you didn't receive and item you paid for, payments made aren't reflected in amounts owed or if your statements are sent to an inaccurate address.

To take advantage of this law, the first thing you need to do is to send a physical letter to the billing inquiries address that the creditor provides. You need to ensure the creditor receives your letter within 60 days from the date the error shows up on your statement. Some creditors allow for disputes to be handled online but utilizing this option can nullify your rights through this law so it is not recommended. The creditor will then have 30 days to acknowledge they received your letter to either correct the mistake or tell you why they think it is valid. If they turn down your request you are then allowed to ask for all the documentation saying why they turned you down.

A subset of this law is what is known as the Hidden Gem Law, this means you can dispute any transaction made within 100 miles of your home, or anywhere in your home state, which exceeds $50. As long as you make a good faith effort to dispute the transaction, and return the item or stop using the service, then the company will likely refund the transaction.

Fair Debt Collection Practices Act: This is another law that benefits consumers when it comes to debt collector actions. This includes not only debt collection agencies but also their attorneys. This law prevents debt collection agencies from contacting you if you have requested that the debt be validated, contacting you instead of your attorney (if applicable) calling before 8 am or after 9 pm, contacting you at work, calling constantly, reporting false information to credit bureaus, embarrassing you in an effort to collect the debt, adding your name to a list of debtors, threatening legal action they can't actually follow through on, misrepresentation or contacting you after you have sent a letter requesting that they stop or saying that you will not pay the debt in question.

If the debt collector breaks these rules or acts in other ways, they are not allowed then you can file a private lawsuit and be recouped costs, fees and damages. What's more, you don't even need to prove damages and you will likely be awarded a minimum of $1,000.

STARTING FROM THE SCRATCH AND MAINTAINING IT

How to Build Credit Score Quickly?

It is nothing but the "score" you accumulate over time and which defines you as a good or bad debtor. I'll explain. If you have a loan of any kind, the more you pay on time and the more your Credit Score goes up if instead, you accumulate delays or unpaid installments your Credit Score drops one round of hell at a time (I think Dante's Inferno he referred to this when he wrote it!)

It is important that you take care of your score consistently because over time it will be the first thing that banks, or loan companies, will see when you ask for a loan to buy a house, a car or anything else. At the moment, it may not seem important but trust me, you will change your mind. I've been there. I didn't give enough importance to it, and when it was time, I regretted it.

The credit card is not the prerogative of Dad's children (except for some cases), but something that young people use to start building their Credit Score from an adolescent age. Unfortunately, we are not 16 years old so we must try to catch up as soon as possible. The problem with the Credit Score is that it is difficult to build when you have no loans or credit cards and it is almost impossible to get either of these if you do not have a Credit Score. In practice, a cat that bites its tail.

How to build a Credit Score from scratch?

There are several ways and all of them are effective.

1.   The first is to open a bank account. Having an account open in itself will not increase your score, but it will give you a starting point to show regular income. After a few months, you can ask your bank (remember to show off your best smile) what services they offer to increase your Credit Score. My bank, for example, offers a mini-loan of $ 500 tied up to be returned in 6 months. It means that you deposit $ 500, they re-loan them to you at a favorable rate and when, in 6 months, you finish paying the installments, they give you back the $ 500 in the barrel. Practically in 6 months, you paid interest as a "tax" with the sole purpose of accumulating points. To put it in simpler words: from 500 and 500 you return, then you pay 500 in installments + interest and you return 500 at the end. It is an expense, but this type of loan guarantees you a considerable accumulation of points, but only if you are regular in payments.

2.   The second, and in my opinion the best, is to apply for a Secured Credit Card. Unlike traditional credit cards, you do not have to show any kind of entry to get approval, but you also have a usage limit. The only thing required is a deposit which is returned to you after a year of regular use. Until a couple of years ago, the deposit was around

200 euros, but with the debt problems that developed after the recession, all the major credit companies have lowered the costs. For example, I applied with Capital One (but there are many others like Discover). The deposit was only $ 49 and the card limit was $ 200 a month with the option of 2% cash back on gas or restaurant expenses. I started using it regularly every month ONLY for these two things and, after a year, my Credit Score was already considered very well, they also returned the deposit and the cash back and the credit limit rose to 500 dollars after only six months. We clarify that you are not obliged to use it only for these things, but I have limited myself for two reasons. The first is to accumulate cash back (i.e., a refund) at the end of the year. The second is to make sure I never use more than 30% of the card limit. Which brings me to the next point.

3. Never exceed 30% of the credit card limit. Believe it or not, it is essential that you show that you do not need a credit card to pay for your things, but that you use it only when strictly necessary or as an accurate choice. The more you use it constantly the better, but judiciously.

4. Pay your installments regularly. All the above points have absolutely no value if you are not constant in payments. No one here scales your loan or credit card debts from your salary. It is your responsibility to remember when you have to pay or set up an automatic payment from your bank account. I decided to set up automatic payments. As long as he has a good memory, you never know what can happen that can put you off your mind on

the expiry day. So, I strongly suggest you do the same because even a missed payment will negatively affect your score.

5. Vary the types of debt as much as you can. If you can make the Secured Card And the mini-loan with the bank at the same time, do it. The more options you have, the faster your Credit Score will grow. Of course, always keep in mind that if you don't pay on time, they show up at home with the Pit bulls (so to speak or almost). So, if you're not sure you can do better, don't risk it and wait a little longer.

6. Add your name to someone else's credit card as an "authorized user". If, for example, if you are married to an American who has had much more time than you to accumulate a decent score (as in my case), it might be a good idea for him to indicate you as an authorized user of his credit cards. This does not mean that you will actually have to use his credit cards, but the more his score improves, the more he will positively influence yours. Be careful though! If you go down, he comes down with you. This type of choice involves a fat, large demonstration of trust so be careful not to betray it. If you mess up the Credit Score that has been sweating so much since he was in swaddling clothes, well I wouldn't want to be in your shoes!

7. Check your Credit Score regularly to make sure there are no problems you are unaware of and have such nasty surprises. Even a late paid bill can affect your payer profile. Now pay attention to the following because it's important. There are several ways to check where you are

with the economic 'pregnancy'. The first is to apply here for your Annual Credit Report, but you are entitled to a free check only once a year. The second is to check directly in Credit Bureaus such as Transunion, Equifax or Experian. Also, in these cases, you can have a free check per year, or pay a monthly installment to keep your score constantly under control. Obviously, the annual checks have their advantages, but be careful not to take too much advantage of their services. Believe it or not, every time you request a check this will lower your Credit Score. Crazy, right? And this brings me to the only sensible solution that remains to keep the score under control.

8. Download the free Credit Karma app. Not only does it constantly give you a detailed report of your score, but also what has positively or negatively influenced, which credit cards or loans are best suited to your situation, your progress, and many other functions. It's all free and, although not updated to the minute, rather accurate. It does not lower your Credit Score and also offers you many other services such as online and free tax returns. Due to Credit Karma, other major credit companies have also had to adjust to offer the Credit Score free check. For example, Capital One and Discover have now integrated this service into their offers (although in a more limited way being a cost to them).

If you follow these tips in a year you can afford to ask for a car loan without having to pay disproportionate interest or even more, depending on your income and your general receivables/payables situation. This reminds me of how important it is to start as soon as possible. Remember that this is the first thing they look at when you need to apply for a loan!

Credit Repair: How to Improve Your Credit Score After Foreclose or Bankruptcy

Regardless of what happened to you financially - if you have gone through foreclosure or bankruptcy, got behind on credit card payments or collected a lot of debt - you can rebuild your credit. Here's how:

Check the credit report

It is determined by a series of factors that can be divided into the following categories: credit history - How long have you been using credit?

How to Apply to For Lines of Credit

You may now have high fico scores, but that is only the beginning. At this point it is all about knowing what to do and where to go to actually turn your credit scores into leveraged money. So now that you have the scores that are needed, where do you go to get the money? If you just want to slowly build your credit up and you are not worried about having access to high credit limits, you can opt-back-in for pre-screened credit offers and apply blindly for whatever offers that may come in the mail, or you can be proactive and come up with a plan.

Going with the flow works perfectly fine for people who are not as concerned or don't take a hands-on approach to building their credit, you will stumble across some quality credit products because these offers will be sent your way, but pre-approvals don't mean you have all the necessary requirements to obtain the actual approval, and I want to save you time by getting you started in the right direction. You might have a few ideas of where you want to apply, but is it the most effective course of action? Have you developed a funding strategy yet? I have no doubt that you will receive offers for 0% balance transfers and a lot of other incentives from companies like Citi Bank, American Express, Discover and a bunch of others, some you will actually get approved for, others will waste your time and deny you. The strategy I am going to show you will allow you to take matters into your own hands and go after what you want as far as credit limits, credit cards with benefits and accounts that will assure you maximum future growth. You want to stay away from any credit cards that will not benefit you down the road because either they lack any substantial reward incentives or room for you to grow the credit limits. You don't want to obtain high credit limits from some, just to be held down by $500 starter credit cards from others just because you were too anxious and excited to get any approval.

HARMING MY CREDIT SCORE

It is also necessary to take a closer look at some of the different parts that are going to end up harming the credit scores that we have. If you are in the process of fixing your credit, you want to make sure that you are careful and that you are not going to end up doing something that will harm your credit in the process. Some of the different things that we are able to watch out for when it comes to harming your credit score include:

Paying Late or Not at All

One of the worst things that you can do when it comes to your credit score is paying late on anything. About 35 percent of your score is going to be about your history of making payments or not on time. Consistently being late on these payments is going to cause a lot of damage to your credit score. Always pay your bills on time, especially your credit card bills.

What is even worse than paying late is not paying at all. If you decide to completely ignore your cards and other bills and not pay them at all, then you are going to be in even more trouble as well. Each month that you miss out on a payment for your credit card, you are going to end up with one month closer to helping your account be charged off.

If you ever want a chance to get your credit score up at all, especially if you are hoping to get it up to 800 or higher, then you have to stop the late payments. This is going to be a bad thing because it shows that you are not willing to pay your money back, and they are less likely to give you some more money in the process.

For those who are struggling with making payments, whether these payments are often late or they don't come in at all, it is time to get a budget in place. You are living above your means, and this is never a good sign to getting your score up to where you would like. When you are able to get your budget in place and can start paying your debts on time, you will be able to get that credit score higher in no time.

Having an Account Charged Off or Sent to Collections

Next on the list is having your accounts charged off. When creditors are worried that you will never pay in your bills for loans or credit cards, they are going to use a process known as charging off your accounts. A charge off means that the insurer has pretty much given up on ever hearing from you again. This is actually one of the absolute worst things out there when it comes to your credit score.

Another issue is when one of your accounts is sent off to collections. Creditors are often going to work with debt collectors in order to work on collecting a payment out of you. Collectors could send your account to collections after, but sometimes before, charging it all off. This is never a good thing, no matter if the account is charged off at that time, either.

If you are to the point of your bills going to collections or being charged off, this means that you have not just missed one or two payments. It means that you have gone so long without paying the whole thing that the company figures they are never going to get it back. They have probably either written it off as a tax break, or they have sold it to a credit collection company that will be bothering you a lot in the future.

Filing Bankruptcy

This is a bit extreme that you should try to avoid at all costs. Bankruptcy is an extreme measure, and it is going to cause a lot of devastation to the score that you are working with. It is also going to be on your record for seven to ten years. It is a good idea to seek some alternatives, like working with counseling for consumer credit, before filing bankruptcy.

It is best if you are able to do everything that you can to avoid bankruptcy at all costs. It may seem like the best idea to work with. You assume that when you declare bankruptcy, you can just walk away from all of the debt that you have, and not have to worry about it ever again. This is not really how this whole process is going to work for you at all, though.

To avoid bankruptcy, you need to go through and learn how to work with a budget and figure out the best ways to manage your money, no matter what the income is that you are working with. The bankruptcy seems like an easy way to get out of the debt, but it haunts you for many years afterward, can make getting credit later on almost impossible, and it will really not solve the underlying problem that got you to this situation.

High Balances or Maxed Out Cards

We always need to take a look at the balances that we are going to have on our credit cards all of the time. The second most important part that comes with our credit score is the amount of debt that is on them, and that is going to be measured out by credit utilization. Having high balances for credit cards, relative to the credit limit that you are working with, will increase the utilization of credit and will make your credit score goes down. For example, if you have a limit of $10,000 on a card, but the balance is at $9500 or higher, then your score is not going to reflect in a positive manner with this one.

We also need to make sure that we are not maxing out or going over the limit when it comes to our credit cards. Credit cards that are over the limit or that have been maxed out are going to make the credit utilization that you have at 100 percent. This is going to be one of the most damaging things that you are able to do with your credit score. Make sure to pay down those debts as fast as you can to maintain your credit score and keep it from going over the top.

Closing Credit Cards

There are a few ways that closing your card is going to end up with a decrease in your credit score. First, we need to take a look at closing up a card that still has a balance on it. When you close that card, the credit limit you get to work with is going to end up at $0, while your balance is still going to be the same. This is going to make it look like you have been able to max out the credit card, which is going to cause your score to drop a bit.

If you want to close your account, then you need to make sure that you pay off the balance before you close it.

What will happen when you close out your credit cards that are old is another thing to study. About 15 percent of your credit score is going to be the length of your credit history, and longer credit histories are going to be better. Closing up old cards, especially some of the oldest cards, are going to make your history seem like it is a lot shorter than it is. Even if you do not use the card anymore, and there are no annual fees, and you should keep the card open because you are really losing nothing and gaining more.

And finally, we need to be careful about closing cards that have available credit. If you have more than one credit card to work with, some that have balanced and some without these, then closing the cards that do not have a balance is going to increase the credit utilization. You can just keep those all out of the way, and see your credit report go up.

Not Having Enough Mix on the Report

While this is not as big of a deal as some of the other options, you will find that having a good mix of credit is going to be about 10 percent of your credit score at the time. If you have a report that only has one or two things on it, such as either credit cards or loans, then it is likely the score you are working with will be affected in some way or another.

The more that you are able to mix up your accounts and get them to have a lot of different things on them, the better. You don't want to overextend yourself, but having a mix of loans, mortgage, credit cards, and more, that you pay off each month without fail, is going to be one of the best ways that you can raise your credit score without causing harm or paying too much in the process.

This is something that often happens; naturally, the longer you work on your credit score. You may have a few credit cards. And then you take out a loan for a car and pay it off. Maybe you need a loan for a vacation or for some home improvement so you will have those accounts. And then get a mortgage too.

Applying for Too Much

Another thing that is going to count on your report is the credit inquiries. These will take up about 10 percent of the score that you work with. Making several applications for loans and credit in a short amount of time is going to cause a big drop in your credit score along the way. Always keep the applications for credit to a minimum, so this doesn't end up harming you along the way.

In some circumstances, this is not going to harm you too much. For example, if you have a good credit score and you want to apply for a mortgage, you will want to apply for a few mortgages and shop around a bit. If you do these close together, then it is not going to be seen as bad because the lender will assume this is what you are doing, rather than you taking on too much or that you have been turned down. You can also explain this to them easily if they ask.

MINDSET OF MONEY MANAGEMENT

The Importance of Money Management

Do you find yourself with different credit cards, a mortgage, and an auto loan?

There are methods to help you make this manageable. It takes time to discover the ins and outs of it and twist your budget so that it can satisfy your needs:

You Know Where Your Money Is Going

This is a huge benefit since it will allow you to watch the way you spend money and save more. You can track your spending for several months and then balance the budget to assign a lot of money to savings, or even retirement.

If you handle your money well, you will manage to make early payments, and avoid surpassing the limit on the credit card.

When you stick to your budget, these methods will assist you to save money.

This prevents you from spending much money.

A Better Plan of Retirement

When you save now and manage your money in the right way, it will benefit you in the long term. First, it will force you to look into the future and look into your retirement plans.

When you implement your money management skills, you will be building yourself a strong retirement plan. The money that you save and invest will grow as time goes by.

Allows You to Concentrate on Your Goals

You will avoid unnecessary expenditure that doesn't support achieving financial goals. If you are dealing with limited resources, budgeting makes it complex to fulfill your ends.

You Organize Your Spending and Savings

When you divide your income into different types of expenditure and savings, a budget will allow you to remain aware of the type of expenditure that drains the portion of your money. This way, it is simple for you to set adjustments. Good money management acts as a reference for organizing receipts, bills, and financial statements. Once you organize all your financial transactions, you will save effort and time.

You Can Speak to Your Partner about Money

If you do share your income with your spouse, then a budget can be the best tool to show how money is spent. This increases teamwork to work on a common financial target and prevents arguments on the way money is used. Creating a budget together with your spouse will help you to avoid conflict and eliminate personal conflicts on the way money is spent.

It Determines Whether You Can Take on Debt and How Much

Taking on debt isn't a bad thing, but it is important, especially if you cannot afford it. A budget will indicate the amount of debt load you can take on without getting stressed.

Budgeting

When you budget, you get the chance to single out and eliminate unnecessary spending such as on penalties, late fees, and interests. These little savings can increase with time.

A budget refers to a plan that takes into account your monthly cash flow and outflow. This is a snapshot of what you own, and what you expect to spend, and which will allow you to realize your financial goals by assisting you in highlighting you're saving and spending.

Creating a budget is the most crucial aspect of financial planning. The amount of money you have doesn't indicate how much money you make, but instead, it is how effective your budgeting is. If you want to take care of your finances, then you will have to understand where your money is flowing to. Contrary to popular belief that budgeting is hard, it isn't, and it doesn't eliminate the fun from your life. A budget will save you from an unexpected financial crisis and a life of debt.

Monitor Your Expenses and Income

The first thing to building a budget is to determine the amount of money you have and what you are spending it on. By monitoring your expenses, you will manage to classify how you spend your money. Planning how you spend your money is critical because you can tell how much you want to spend in every category. You can monitor your income and expenses by creating a journal, spreadsheet, or cash book. Every time you make money, you can monitor it as income, and every time you spend money, you can track it as an expense.

If you use a debit card, try to track back three months of your spending to get a comprehensive picture of your expenditure.

Evaluate Your Income

The next stage is to assess your income. You can do this by computing the amount of income you get via gifts, scholarships, etc.

Determine Your Expenses

Once you know your monthly income, next is to determine the total of your expenses. First, you need to define what your fixed, variable expenses are. Fixed expenses, sales, and bills have the same price every month. The fixed expenses comprise of car payments, internet, and rent. Variable expenses refer to costs that change, such as utilities and groceries.

Be sure to include payments of debt in your budget. Find out the amount that you can contribute towards your debts to make sure that you are on the correct path to financial stability. Handling debts and savings go hand in hand.

Building a Saving Strategy

It is quite easy to forget to save money. Keep in mind that you always pay yourself first. Give it a try using 10-20% of your income savings. Since savings increase, you can choose to include money that you didn't spend in the budget to save.

Many people know how to manage the little money they get when the month ends, but they find it hard to save when they have a tight budget. If you look at finance articles online, you will see different types of saving methods—right from freezing all spending to packing your own lunch for a month. But how can you determine which one's work? In this part, you will learn easy money-saving strategies you can implement and how you can make them work for you:

Stay Out of Debt

Being debt free will help you to save cash; if you can pay off all your debt, you will get the chance to organize your debt.

The stats on eliminating debt can be shocking. For example, the Claris poll showed that only 22% of people attempted this strategy, and 26% reported that it worked for them. In other words, this strategy can help you save money.

Staying out of debt can save you a good sum of cash, but many people find it hard to pay off their debts.

Be a Minimalist

Adopting a minimalist approach is a type of voluntary simplicity. It requires a person to cut down on costs so that they concentrate on what is important. A minimalist's life generally means owning smaller house, fewer "toys", and fewer clothes. But it also implies minimal work and more time to do the things that you like.

This is a great saving strategy that works even for those who don't want to use it. A minimalist approach can be the effect of other methods to save. In most cases, many people scaled their life to stick to their budget. Then, with time, they discovered that their simple lifestyle helped them save more.

There are various misconceptions about minimalism. A blog about minimalism jokes that minimalists live in small apartments and don't have jobs, cars, TVs, or more than 100 objects.

The purpose of minimalism is to free yourself from issues in life that aren't important. It is not focused on sacrifice; it merely involves eliminating things that you don't want to have in life or creating room for things that you care about. As a result, living with fewer items can make you feel satisfied.

If you aren't sure whether you can deal with this kind of life, you can start small and slowly identify a few things in your life that you don't want. For example, if your wardrobe is filled with many things, perhaps throw out or donate some clothes. Or if you spend a lot of time online, plan to reduce your screen time.

Whatever you decide to do, make sure that you don't simplify your life by surrendering on the things you value or treasure;

instead, choose things that require the most work for the least reward.

Since they have worked for other people, there is a big chance that they will work for you too. However, make sure that you don't jump in and try all the methods at once—just select strategies that you believe may work for you.

Investing your Money

Investing your money gives you a chance to grow your money, and even make more than what you have. However, not everyone who decides to invest their money makes profits; some have lost tons of money in the process. There is a different way to invest your money, and this will introduce you to some of the most common strategies for investment:

Online investing can be a quick and convenient method that is more affordable than other methods. But before you can handle your online investment, you need to ask yourself several questions:

Online investing is designed for everyone. By choosing this option, you hold the responsibility to research all investments and make all investment decisions regarding your online account. If you don't feel okay as that kind of investor, you could be comfortable working with a financial advisor. If you like to manage your investment portfolio and feel secure that you have enough knowledge, you may decide to go with online investment.

Stop Spending

If you can't stop spending money that you don't have, this book will only temporarily fix your problems, if it is even able to do that. If you have a habit of living out of your means and buying things you cannot afford, this is your chance to fix that. If you want to fix your credit and improve your life financially, you must take care of these things. So, sit tight, make a budget, and find something that works, and cut up those maxed out credit cards if you have to.

BONUS CHAPTER: 609 TEMPLATES

Letter #1

(Initial Letter to Credit Bureau Disputing Items)

{Name of Bureau}

{Address}

{Date}

{Name on account}

{Report number}

To whom it may concern:

On {Date of Credit Report} I received a copy of my credit report which contains errors that are damaging to my credit score. I am requesting the following items be completely investigated as each account contains several mistakes.

{Creditor 1 / Account number}

{Creditor 2 / Account number}

{Creditor 3 / Account number}

Thank you in advance for your time. I understand that you need to check with the original creditors on these accounts and that you will make sure every detail is accurate. I also understand that under the Fair Credit Reporting Act you will need to complete your investigation within 30 days of receiving this letter. Once you are finished with your investigation, please send me a copy of my new credit report showing the changes. Looking forward to hear from you as I am actively looking for a new job and wouldn't want these mistakes on my credit report to stand in my way.

Sincerely,

{Your signature}

{Your Printed Name}

{Your Address}

{Your Phone Number}

{Your Social Security Number}

Attach a copy of the credit report showing which accounts you are disputing

Letter #2

(When you don't get a response from Letter #1)

{Name of Bureau}

{Address}

{Date}

{Name on account}

{Report number}

To whom it may concern:

On {Date of your first letter} I sent you a letter asking you to investigate several mistakes on my credit report. I've included a copy of my first letter and a copy of the report with the mistakes circled. The Fair Credit Reporting Act says I should only have to wait 30 days for the investigation to be finished. It has been more than 30 days and I still have not heard anything.

I'm guessing that since you have not responded that you were not able to verify the information on the mistaken accounts. Since it has been more than 30 days, please remove the mistakes from my credit report and send me a copy of my updated credit report. Also, as required by law, please send an updated copy of my credit report to anyone who requested a copy of my credit file in the past six months.

Looking forward to hear from you as I am actively looking for a new job and wouldn't want these mistakes on my credit report to stand in my way.

Sincerely,

{Your signature}

{Your Printed Name}

{Your Address}

{Your Phone Number}

{Your Social Security Number}

Attach a copy of the credit report showing which accounts you are disputing

Attach a copy of your original letter

Attach a copy of the registered letter receipts showing the date they received your original letter

Letter #3

(Request for removal of negative items from original creditor)

{Name of Creditor}

{Address}

{Date}

{Name on account}

To whom it may concern:

On {Date of Credit Report} I received a copy of my credit report which contains errors that are damaging to my credit score. I am requesting the following items be completely investigated as each account contains several mistakes.

{Description of item(s) you are disputing/account number(s)}

I have enclosed a duplicate of the credit report and have highlighted the account(s) in question.

Thank you in advance for your time. I understand that you need to check on these accounts and that you will make sure every detail is accurate. I also understand that under the Fair Credit Reporting Act you will need to complete your investigation within 30 days of receiving this letter. Once you are finished with your investigation, please alert all major credit bureaus where you have reported my information. Also, please send me a letter confirming the changes.

Looking forward to hear from you as I am actively looking for a new job and wouldn't want these mistakes on my credit report to stand in my way.

Sincerely,

{Your signature}

{Your Printed Name}

{Your Address}

{Your Phone Number}

{Your Social Security Number}

Attach a copy of the credit report showing which accounts you are disputing

Letter #4

(If you don't receive a response from Letter #3)

{Name of Creditor}

{Address}

{Date}

{Name on account}

To whom it may concern:

On {Date of your first letter} I sent you a letter asking you to investigate several mistakes on my credit report. I've included a copy of my first letter and a copy of the report with the mistakes circled. The Fair Credit Reporting Act says I should only have to wait 30 days for the investigation to be finished. It has been more than 30 days and I still have not heard anything.

I'm guessing that since you have not responded that you were not able to verify the information on the mistaken accounts. Since it has been more than 30 days, please immediately report the updated information to all major credit bureaus so they may update my credit report. Also, please send me a letter confirming these changes to the way you report my account.

Looking forward to hear from you as I am actively looking for a new job and wouldn't want these mistakes on my credit report to stand in my way.

Sincerely,

{Your signature}

{Your Printed Name}

{Your Address}

{Your Phone Number}

{Your Social Security Number}

Attach a copy of the credit report showing which accounts you are disputing

Attach a copy of your original letter

Attach a copy of the registered letter receipts showing the date they received your original letter

Letter #5

(If the Credit Bureau doesn't remove negative items disputed)

{Name of Credit Bureau}

{Address}

{Date}

{Name on account}

{Report number}

To whom it may concern:

On {Date of your first letter} I sent you a letter asking you to investigate several mistakes on my credit report. I've included a copy of my first letter and a copy of the report with the mistakes circled. According to your response you have chosen to leave these negative items on my credit report adding insult to injury. The items in question are:

{Creditor 1 / Account number}

{Creditor 2 / Account number}

{Creditor 3 / Account number}

I find it completely unacceptable that you and the creditor refuse to properly investigate my dispute. Your refusal to follow the Fair Credit Reporting Act is causing me untold stress and anxiety. Since you won't follow through, I want to know exactly how you investigated each account. Therefore, I would like the name, title and contact information for the person at the creditor with whom you did the investigation. This will let me personally follow up with the creditor and find out why they are choosing to report these mistakes on my credit month after month.

I see I am only one person among thousands or more that you have to look after, but to me this is both personally damaging and humiliating. You may not understand it and you don't have to--all I'm asking is that when people look at my credit file, they see the most accurate information and that's not what's happening.

Please provide me with the requested information right away so I can finally put this nightmare behind me.

Looking forward to hear from you as I am actively looking for a new job and wouldn't want these mistakes on my credit report to stand in my way.

Sincerely,

{Your signature}

{Your Printed Name}

{Your Address}

{Your Phone Number}

{Your Social Security Number}

Attach a copy of the credit report showing which accounts you are disputing

Attach a copy of your original letter

Attach a copy of the Bureau's response showing no changes to your credit

Letter 6: Affidavit of Unknown Inquiries

EQUIFAX

P.O. box 740256

ATLANTA GA 30374

My name Is John William; my current address is 6767. W Phillips Road, San Jose, CA 78536, SSN: 454-02-9928, Phone: 415-982-3426, Birthdate: 6-5-1981

I checked my credit reports and noticed some inquiries from companies that I did not give consent to access my credit reports; I am very concerned about all activity going on with my credit reports these days. I immediately demand the removal of these inquiries to avoid any confusion as I DID NOT initiate these inquires or give any form of consent electronically, in person, or over the phone. I am fully aware that without permissible purpose no entity is allowed to pull my credit unless otherwise noted in section 604 of the FCRA.

The following companies did not have permission to request my credit report:

CUDL/FIRST CALIFORNIA ON 6-15-2017

CUDL/NASA FEDERAL CREDIT UNION ON 6-15-2017

LOANME INC 3-14-2016

CBNA on 12-22-2017

I once again demand the removal of these unauthorized inquiries immediately.

THANK YOU

(Signature)

Letter 7: Affidavit of Suspicious Addresses

1-30-2018

ASHLEY WHITE

2221 N ORANGE AVE APT 199

FRESNO CA 93727

PHONE: 559-312-0997

SSN: 555-59-4444

BIRTHDATE: 4-20-1979

EQUIFAX

P.O. box 740256

ATLANTA GA 30374

To whom it may concern:

I recently checked a copy of my credit report and noticed some addresses reporting that do not belong to me or have been obsolete for an extended period of time. For the safety of my information, I hereby request that the following obsolete addresses be deleted from my credit reports immediately;

4488 N white Ave apt 840 Fresno, CA 93722

4444 W Brown Ave apt 1027 Fresno CA 93722

13330 E Blue Ave Apt 189 Fresno CA 93706

I have provided my identification card and social security card to verify my identity and current address. Please notify any creditors who may be reporting any unauthorized past accounts that are in connection with these mentioned addresses as I have exhausted all of my options with the furnishers.

(Your signature)

This letter is to get a response from the courts to show the credit bureaus that you have evidence that they cannot legally validate the Bankruptcy

Letter 8: Affidavit of James Robert

U.S BANKRUPTCY COURT

700 STEWART STREET 6301

SEATTLE, WA 98101

RE: BANKRUPTCY (164444423TWD SEATTLE, WA)

To whom it may concern:

My Name is JAMES ROBERT my mailing address is 9631 s 2099h CT Kent, WA 99999.

I recently reviewed my credit reports and came upon the above referenced public record. The credit agencies have been contacted and they report in their investigation that you furnished or reported to them that the above matter belongs to me. This act may have violated federal and Washington state privacy laws by submitting such information directly to the credit agencies, Experian, Equifax, and Transunion via mail, phone or fax.

I wish to know if your office violated Washington State and federal privacy laws by providing information on the above referenced matter via phone, fax or mail to Equifax, Experian or Transunion.

Please respond as I have included a self-addressed envelope,

Thank You

(Your signature)

Letter 9: Affidavit of Erroneous Entry

Dispute letter for bankruptcy to credit bureaus

1-1-18

JAMES LEE

131 S 208TH CT

KENT WA 98031

SSN: 655-88-0000

PHONE: 516-637-5659

BIRTHDATE: 10-29-1985

EXPERIAN

P. O. Box 4500

Allen, TX 75013

RE: BANKRUPTCY (132323993TWD SEATTLE, WA)

To whom it may concern:

My Name is James LEE my mailing address is 131 s 208th CT Kent, WA 98031

I recently disputed the entry of a bankruptcy that shows on my credit report which concluded as a verified entry your bureau. I hereby request your methods of verification, if my request cannot be met, I demand that you delete this entry right away and submit me an updated credit report showing the changes.

Thank You

(Your signature)

Letter10: Affidavit for Account Validation

First letter you send to the credit bureaus for disputes

1-18-2019

TRANSUNION

P.O. BOX 2000

CHESTER PA 19016

To Whom It May Concern:

My name is John Doe, SSN: 234-76-8989, my current address is 4534. N Folk street Victorville, CA 67378, Phone: 310-672-0929 and I was born on 4-22-1988.

After checking my credit report, I have found a few accounts listed above that I do not recognize. I understand that before any account or information can be furnished to the credit bureaus; all information and all accounts must be 100% accurate, verifiable and properly validated. I am not disputing the existence of this debt, but I am denying that I am the responsible debtor. I am also aware that mistakes happen, I believe these accounts can belong to someone else with a similar name or with my information used without my consent either from the furnisher itself or an individual.

I am demanding physical documents with my signature or any legally binding instruments that can prove my connection to these erroneous entries, Failure to fully verify that these accounts are accurate is a violation of the FCRA and must be removed or it will continue to damage my ability to obtain additional credit from this point forward.

I hereby demand that the accounts listed above be legally validated or be removed from my credit report immediately.

Thank You

(Your signature)

Letter 11: Affidavit of Request for Method Verification

Second letter to Credit Bureau if they verified anything

10-22-17

JOSHUA ETHAN

2424 E Dawn Hill way

Merced, CA 93245

SSN: 555-22-3333

Phone: 415-222-9090

Birthdate: 9-29-1987

EQUIFAX

P.O. BOX 740256

ATLANTA GA 30374

To whom it may concern:

I recently submitted a request for investigation on the following accounts which were determined as verified:

Acct Numbers# (XXXXXXX COLLECTION AGENCY A)

(XXXXXXX COLLECTION AGENCY B)

I submitted enough information for you to carry out a reasonable investigation of my dispute, you did not investigate this account or account(s) thoroughly enough as you chose to verify the disputed items.

Under section 611 of the FCRA I hereby request the methods in which you verified these entries. If you cannot provide me with a reasonable reinvestigation and the methods of which you used for verification, please delete these erroneous entries from my credit report. Furthermore, I would like to be presented with all relevant documents pertaining to the disputed entries.

I look forward to resolving this manner

(Your signature)

Letter 12: Affidavit for Validation

This is the first letter sent to the collection agency if the account is already on your credit reports

1-22-2017

JAMES DANIEL

13233 ROYAL LANDS

LAS VEGAS NV 89141

SSN: 600-60-0003

BIRTHDATE: 2-18-1991

PHONE: 702-331-3912

EXPERIAN

P. O. BOX 4500

ALLEN, TX 75013

To Whom It May Concern:

After reviewing my credit reports, I noticed this unknown item that you must have furnished in error, I formally deny being responsible for any parts of this debt.

Please send me any and all copies of the original documentation that legally binds me to this account, also including the true ownership of this debt.

This account is unknown to me and I formally ask that your entity cease all reporting of this account to the credit agencies and cease all collection attempts.

ACCOUNT: UNIVERSITY OF PHOENIX (IRN 9042029892)

If you cannot present what I request, I demand you stop reporting this account to the credit bureaus to avoid FCRA and FDCPA violations and cease all contact efforts and debt collection activity.

Please respond in writing within 30 days so we can resolve this matter without any more violations.

Thank you. (Your signature)

Letter 13: Affidavit of Method Verification

Second letter to collection agency if they verified anything

1-30-2018

JAMES DAVID

1111 N FAIR AVE APT 101

FRESNO CA 93706

PHONE: 559-399-0999

SSN: 555-59-5599

BIRTHDATE: 9-25-1979

EXPERIAN

P. O. BOX 4500

ALLEN, TX 75013

To Whom It May Concern:

I previously disputed this account with your company and it resulted in you verifying this entry. I am once again demanding validation of this debt for the second time as I have yet to receive sufficient documentation that legally shows I am responsible for this matter.

In addition to requesting validation, I am formally requesting your method of verification for these entries that I have previously disputed, please supply me with any documentation you may have on file to aid your stance.

If this entry cannot be validated or if the method of verification cannot be provided to me in a timely manner, I demand that you delete this entry immediately.

Thank you. (Your signature)

Letter 14: Affidavit of Fraudulent Information

Letter to Credit Bureau for identity theft

10-17-17

HELEN JOHNSON

2525 S CHERRY AVE APT 201

FRESNO, CA 93702

PHONE 559-299-2328

BIRTHDAY 11-30-1990

SOCIAL SECURITY NUMBER 555-89-1111

EQUIFAX CONSUMER

FRAUD DIVISION

P.O. BOX 740256

ATLANTA GA 30374

To whom it may concern:

I am writing this letter to document all of the accounts reported by these furnishers that stem from identity theft. I have read and understand every right I have under section 605B and section 609 of the FCRA. Please block the following accounts that are crippling my consumer reports as I do not recognize, nor am I responsible for, nor have I received any money or goods from the creation of these unknown accounts.

Please refer to Police Report and ID Theft Affidavit attached.

1) CBE GROUP (12323239XXXX)

2) LOBEL FINANCIAL (431XXXX)

Please contact each credit to prevent further charges, activity, or authorizations of any sort regarding my personal information.

Thank you

(Your signature)

Letter 15: Affidavit of fraudulent information

Letter to lender or collection agency when reporting fraudulent accounts

10-15-17

TARA BROWN

3421 N ROSE AVE APT 211

OAKLAND CA 93766

PHONE 559-369-9999

BIRTHDAY 9-20-1979

SOCIAL SECURITY NUMBER 584-00-0222

MONTGOMERY WARD

RE Account # 722222XXXX

TRANSUNION

P.O. BOX 2000

CHESTER PA 19016

To whom it may concern:

I have recently reviewed my credit reports and found an account listed that I do not recognize. I am informing you today that you are reporting the above-mentioned account that is a result of identity theft, and continuing to report this entry will be in violation under FACTA rules and regulations.

I have never had this account MONTGOMERY WARD 99986518XXXX, I ask that you to cease all reporting and collection activity surrounding this account which is my right under section 605B of the FCRA, please refer to police report.

I ask that this information be blocked and disregarded from your accounting. Thank you for your time and I will be eagerly waiting for your response.

Thank You

(Your signature)